RESISTING READING MANDATES

How to Triumph with the Truth

Elaine M. Garan

HEINEMANN
Portsmouth, NH

Heinemann
A division of Reed Elsevier Inc.
361 Hanover Street
Portsmouth, NH 03801–3912
www.heinemann.com

Offices and agents throughout the world

Library of Congress Cataloging-in-Publication Data
Garan, Elaine M.
    Resisting reading mandates : how to triumph with the truth /
Elaine M. Garan
        p. cm.
    Includes bibliographical references and index.
    ISBN 0-325-00446-3 (alk. paper)
    1. Reading—Phonetic method—United States.   2. National Reading
Panel (U.S.)—Evaluation.   3. Education and state—United States.
I. Title.

LB1573.3 .G35 2002
372.46'5—dc21

                                                                    2001051790

Editor: Lois Bridges
Production: Elizabeth Valway
Cover design: Linda Knowles
Typesetter: PD&PS
Manufacturing: Steve Bernier

Printed in the United States of America on acid-free paper
06 05 04 03   VP   3 4 5

CONTENTS

For children.
They truly believe we will do the right thing.

FOREWORD

Outside my university office door I have posted a lapel button that is imprinted with the message: "Sed quis custodiet ipsos custodes?" Literally translated this Latin quote asks: But who will guard the guards?

That seems an entirely appropriate question for educators to be considering these days. It is a question central to the primary argument Elaine Garan sets forth in this small but important book. Who should monitor the reliability of summaries of "what the research says"? This is a question I've raised recently regarding some of the preposterous assertions made about the research on the utility of decodable texts. There is no research base supporting the use of decodable texts regardless of the many assertions to the contrary made in documents published by the California Department of Education, the Texas Education Agency, and the Learning First Alliance (see Allington 1999; Allington and Woodside-Jiron 1998a, 1999).

But now it isn't just state policy actors who are distorting what the research says. Now, as Garan so carefully documents here, we have a report, sponsored and distributed by federal agencies, making assertions about what the research says—a report that distorts and misrepresents the findings of the National Reading Panel. Further, Garan shows that even the original findings of the National Reading Panel have been challenged by leading researchers on methodological and conceptual grounds.

Does it matter? And if it does, what should we as professionals do?

It does matter, and it matters on a variety of levels. As a researcher, I don't need anyone providing more evidence suggesting, ultimately, that educational research is an untrustworthy basis for improving teaching and learning. And that is just what happens when ideological tracts trump reliable research summaries.

It matters to teachers and administrators who don't need ideological faddism dominating educational policy making. Improving teaching and learning in the real world of schools and classrooms is difficult enough without government-sponsored misallocation of effort and funding.

It matters to parents and taxpayers. Parents, because it is your children who will fail to profit from ideological policy making while some profit financially. Taxpayers, because it is your tax dollars that support the ideological faddism being so heavily promoted in recent federal programs and legislation—tax dollars that might be working to improve the quality of education in your community instead.

There is no real argument about whether good readers need to develop rapid, accurate decoding proficiencies. They do. The questions rage around the issue of how to develop these proficiencies. That is where the faddism rears its increasingly ugly head. And it gets worse.

The misinformation campaign focuses not only on misrepresenting what we know about how to best develop decoding proficiency, but also supports the notion that educators are ignoring what the research says. Thus, the misinformation campaign works to undermine public confidence in educators and to disenfranchise local control of education by mandating methodology from afar.

This seems serious to me. It seems serious to Elaine Garan.

Elaine has produced an incredibly useful book here. She has dissected the five hundred-page National Reading Panel Report and the Summary of that report, which so incredibly misrepresents the panel report. She provides a practical reference tool for us to use whenever anyone attempts to promote these misrepresentations as a basis for educational policy mandates.

This plain-language explanation of what has been misrepresented in the research on teaching beginning reading is a good start in what, I hope, becomes a widespread campaign to expose the faddists and ideologues and return to reform efforts that are based on reliable research about good teaching of reading. But you must contribute to the effort by passing this book along to colleagues, administrators, board members, policy makers, and media. Use it to argue against faddism in the name of science. Use it to reassure yourself that much of what you've known about good teaching is not antiscientific. But use it you must. We must all share the responsibility and guard the guards.

Dick Allington
University of Florida

ACKNOWLEDGMENTS

The Report of the National Reading Panel (NRP) is a shamelessly flawed research effort. Nevertheless, it has inflicted and will continue to inflict tremendous harm on the field of reading and, more important, on children. The report has also served as the catalyst for many of us to crystallize our beliefs. In an odd way, then, I am grateful to the NRP. As a result of its report, I am now in contact with a number of people whom I previously admired from afar, including the incredible Regie Routman, who won't be silenced in her crusade to help teachers and children. And because of the NRP, I've benefited firsthand from the tireless contributions and generosity of Steve Krashen, who has helped me every step of the way in my efforts to expose the errors in the report. He is an inspiration for us all. Thanks to the NRP, I now count Steve as a personal friend.

When I first started on my analysis, Jack Benninga, the chair of my department at California State University–Fresno, listened to me daily as I unearthed error after error in the NRP report, and it was he who encouraged me to send the article to *Phi Delta Kappan*. Jack did everything but dance down the hall when my articles were accepted. Our dean of education, Paul Shaker, also helped me face the fears I had of political reprisals from the State of California. He has always encouraged us to take a public stand on issues even when they didn't agree with his own views.

And if it weren't for the NRP report, Lois Bridges at Heinemann would only be a name that I've seen in other authors' acknowledgments. She is a rare person, who knows who she is and what she stands for and is unwavering in her efforts on behalf of children. Anytime I was discouraged and felt like giving up, Lois was there to make sure I kept going. I am grateful to have the honor of counting her as editor and friend.

Two lifelong friends, who have changed my life, have served as personal and professional models for me and are as incredibly brave and uncompromising in their integrity as I wish I could always be. Mary Shea lost sleep helping me through our doctoral program and is still always there for me. And nearly everything I have accomplished professionally traces back directly to Ardith Cole. She opened my eyes in so many ways. She is the consummate teacher, mentor, and friend. Ardie also risked my wrath to courageously edit just about everything I've ever written, in spite of the fact that I wax grateful only when it is all over—and am relentlessly nasty until it is.

I am also grateful to all the wonderful people who never give up and who have never been silenced—or silent—when it comes to fighting for the rights of children. You know who you are.

Finally, I owe everything I am to my parents, Eugene and Elizabeth Garan. They always stood up for what was right and taught me to do the same.

ABOUT THIS BOOK

Dear Teachers,

This book is for you. It evolved as a result of questions that many of you are asking about the current pressures to teach isolated phonics and phonemic awareness, particularly through the use of commercial programs. We've all heard the conflicting research claims as opposing factions in the phonics wars try to convince us that their philosophy and their methods are best.

In the past, many of us were able to resist the idea of research-driven directives from outside our own classrooms, our own schools, and even our own communities. We could just shut the doors to our classrooms and teach the way our hearts and our professional expertise told us was right. Even though we could feel the maelstrom swirling about our heads, for the most part we could just ignore it. Unfortunately, that time is past. Increasingly, people who have never even set foot in our classrooms and who do not know our students are telling us how to teach them. Often, we as teachers are not even participants in the conversation as we are silenced by the words, "You must teach this. You must use this program. You must follow this script because *scientific research says you should*. This book will enable you to respond to the "research says" claims.

Why can't we just ignore the outside pressures anymore?

We are now experiencing unprecedented pressure from all directions, from parents and administrators, from organized community groups, and from "faith" groups with a variety of religious affiliations and personal agendas. These groups are well-meaning and most are sincerely committed to doing what they believe is best for children. However, such groups may be particularly vulnerable to the promises of "experts" outside the classroom. Any concerned parent who picks up a newspaper or turns on the nightly news is bombarded with the propaganda designed to convince us all that the education system in this country has failed.

Educators have always been vulnerable to criticism, but now more than ever the news media have targeted schools and teachers as convenient scapegoats for the ills of society. Newspapers publish test scores and vilify us in the name of accountability and higher standards, and as we know, such negative, public censure is frequently based on false information. The barrage of criticism is so relentless that sometimes even we ourselves become convinced that "experts" outside our own classrooms know more about teaching than we do. Our confidence in our role as professionals, as well as our ability to make curriculum decisions, gradually erodes and we sometimes forget how good we really are.

Today another very powerful outside faction has joined the attack on schools and teachers. The federal government has decided it knows better than we do—*what* we should teach, *how* we should teach, and even *when* we should teach it. What teacher in this country hasn't experienced the pressure of high-stakes testing, the results of which are linked not only to the placement and promotion of our children but to the distribution of funding for schools as well? In some places, even teachers' and administrators' salaries are impacted by students' performance on standardized tests, sometimes based on as little as a single score.[1]

And so today, we are up against yet another one-size-fits-all, surefire, quick fix. The United States government is now inside our classrooms as we are pressured to follow the "proven" methods recommended by *the* research. The latest buzzword is "science"—

and it is a force to be reckoned with. The powerful document that is usurping our expertise as professionals is *The Report of the National Reading Panel: Teaching Children to Read*, often referred to as the NRP report. It is the so-called "scientific" research of the NRP that drives the recommendations of President Bush's education plan, *No Child Left Behind*.[2A]

THE BUSH EDUCATION PLAN

How can the Bush Education Plan regulate what I teach?

At the heart of the Bush plan is the old-fashioned carrot and stick. The carrot in the Bush plan is the promise of grants and other monetary benefits to those schools that get in line and use the science. The big stick in the plan, of course, is that funding for schools, and even our salaries, are threatened if we fail to comply with the NRP's back-to-basics focus on isolated skill and drill.[2B]

Coincidentally, such regimented skills instruction means big money for big publishers. McGraw-Hill, for example, is echoing the words of the Bush Education Plan in its sales promotions and promises. Attend one of McGraw-Hill's presentations at a reading conference and you will hear the very words of the Bush Education Plan echoed in its slick high-tech sales pitch: "Just use our science-based, Open Court reading program and no child will be left behind—*not one*. Just use Open Court," they claim, "and *every* child in your care will be a competent reader—every single one."[3] What enormous pressure there is for us to buy government-supported science.[4] And think about this: If the *science* is infallible and yet some children still fail, then who is to blame? We, the teachers are. If you haven't felt the influence of the NRP yet, you will.

BACKGROUND AND PURPOSE OF THE NRP

What is the Report of the National Reading Panel and what was its purpose?

In 1997, The National Institute for Child Health and Human Development (NICHD) appointed a National Reading Panel (NRP). Oddly enough, the majority of the fourteen-member panel had never been directly involved in actually teaching children to read but came from an unusual assortment of occupations. These included a certified public accountant, a physics professor, a neuroscientist, an assistant director of the National Science Foundation, a director of urban education, and seven cognitive psychologist/scientists. Only two panel members had close links to the actual teaching of reading. Mrs. Gwenette Ferguson was the only reading teacher on the panel.[5] Dr. Joanne Yatvin is an award-winning teacher and principal and has forty-one years of experience as a classroom teacher and school administrator. It is she who first protested the credibility of the panel and wrote a minority report. In spite of the lack of classroom teaching experience that characterized the backgrounds of most panel members, their mission was to review the field of literature related to reading instruction, analyze it using a *medical* research model, and formulate a strategy for changing our classrooms based on the results of its "science."[6]

What does the National Reading Panel mean by "science"? What can medicine possibly have to do with teaching reading?

This is not by any means a textbook on research, and I'm not offering any lengthy explanations of research terminology here, for that is not my purpose. However, I will provide some very basic background information about the NRP report that may be useful, particularly in determining what the report means by the term *science*. We must rob that word of its mystery in order to combat it, for so-called scientific, infallible reading methods are coming to our classrooms.

The work of the National Reading Panel all begins and ends with the notion that reading is scientific, a series of isolated skills that can be identified, measured, put together, and ultimately taught according to a prescribed, sequential formula. The thinking goes something like this: Since reading (so the scientists on the panel believe) is comprised of discrete skills, a series of easy-to-measure bits and pieces, then it is possible to draw legitimate research parallels between reading and experiments used in the field of medicine. This means that the methods used for the panel's research "include behaviorally based interventions, medications, or medical procedures proposed for use in the fostering of robust health and psychological development and the prevention of disease."[7] I know it is hard to believe, but the previous quote is taken directly from the NRP and was written by the people the government has designated as "experts" on reading.

Perhaps you are wondering how the panel could possibly compare research on children's reading to research on medications and the prevention of disease. The answer to this question may lie in the makeup of the panel members. As we have seen, the majority of the panel members were *not* classroom teachers who know and understand children and the complexities of the reading process. Most were cognitive psychologists or scientists who never taught children to read themselves but were nevertheless selected to inform *real* teachers how to do it. As a result, the studies the panel chose to include in its analysis used "experimental" methods. The NRP claimed it included only studies that used *treatment groups* (in which children were trained in an isolated reading skill) and *control groups* (in which children were not trained in the same isolated skill as the treatment group). In point of fact, the panel made arbitrary decisions to include the findings of research using other methods.[8] We will discuss the implications of the inconsistency among research methods later in the book.

For now, I'll provide a description of how experimental studies work. In a nutshell, children are divided into two groups. The treatment group is trained in a particular skill or method and is compared to the control group, children who are not trained in the skill that is being assessed. At the beginning of the training period, the researchers give both the treatment and control groups a pretest. At the end of the training period, both groups are tested again. The results of the posttest are compared to the pretest scores to see which group learned the skill better. Those of us who actually teach can see the flaw in the National Reading Panel's medical model: Because the NRP focused its research on isolated skills, they ignored the complexities of the reading process, as well as the incredible complexities of real children in real classrooms. In fact, only about 16 percent of the studies in the phonics report even looked at the impact of its scientific methods on children's reading comprehension of authentic, connected text.[9]

Regardless of our own personal philosophies, don't we all pretty much agree that *comprehension* is a vital outcome of the reading process? Who among us would claim that the purpose of reading is the ability to sound out words without any consideration as to whether or not the child understands the meaning of text or even the isolated words themselves? Have you known children who could decode beautifully and give the impression of reading while not comprehending the text at all? I know I have.

At this point, it's tempting to say, "The *Report of the National Reading Panel* is irrelevant." I would agree except for one harsh reality. You will recall that President Bush's Education Plan, *No Child Left Behind,* is based on the findings of the National Reading Panel. You will recall also that the goal of the Bush plan is to force us all to comply with the results of the NRP's medical research model and to implement its scientific methods in our classrooms. Therefore, as much as we would like to just shut our doors until this latest imposition on our teaching goes away, we can't. The NRP is not just some pesky little mosquito buzzing in our ears. It is Godzilla and it has its foot on our heads. Like it or not, we must deal with the findings of the National Reading Panel. And so we shall, by meeting them on their own ground.

What can teachers answer when they are told that they must implement research-based methods and programs in their classrooms?

The NRP report is an overwhelming document, over five hundred pages in length. It uses tables, statistics, and research terminology foreign to many of us teachers who are intensely involved in actually teaching children and cannot dedicate the many hours needed to make sense of the NRP findings. Even many university professors do not have the quantitative statistical background to "talk back" to the barrage of jargon that obscures the findings of the report.

This book gives you some handy tools to defend your own beliefs and your own professional autonomy. You don't have to compile reams of your own research to argue against the science and results of the report. Quite the contrary. Believe it or not, you can use the National Reading Panel's own findings to defend your rights as teachers and to protect the children in your care from expensive programs based on false research claims.

This book will empower you. It will enable you to hold a mirror to the scientific claims made in the Bush Education Plan and refute them using the National Reading Panel's own words. To that end, responses to the questions in this book are limited to the NRP's own findings and to other research that has been validated by the NRP or by the assistant secretary of education, Susan Neuman. That is, I will not bombard you with a lot of other supportive research not included in the report itself. By adhering strictly to the NRP's research *or* to research validated as being "scientific" by government representatives, we have put "them" in an untenable position. If they dispute the carefully documented facts I provide here, they will have to bite their own tails. How can they argue against their own science?

The National Reading Panel deliberately excluded a large, widely respected body of research from its analysis because such studies did not conform to their scientific, medical model. The fact that I don't discuss these studies doesn't mean that I don't value and respect such research, nor does my exclusion of findings mean that I hope you will ignore research beyond the NRP, as it can legitimately inform your classroom practice. But before we can get to that point, we must deal with the challenge of the panel's science, for that is what many factions are thrusting upon us.

My point is, "they" want science, so we will give them science! Together we will learn to talk back to the scientific experts in their own language, using their own findings. The mirror we hold up will blind them with their own science. I promise.

HOW TO USE THIS BOOK

This book is based on a question-and-answer format that will make it easy for you to reference. I have solicited questions from classroom teachers around the country. The table of contents lists the topics covered by the questions in the book. The questions cover teaching comprehension, spelling, phonics, and phonemic awareness, as well as the value of specific commercial programs such as Open Court and Direct Instruction. First, I answer each question in plain English and *always* based on the findings of the National Reading Panel or on research validated as being scientific by agents for the Bush administration. Following my de-jargonized answer, I cite the exact quote, including chapter and page number, from the NRP report—in case you need to defend your practices to critics. Other references will be footnoted. Those endnotes are there for your convenience. You can refer to them to support every statement I make in this book.

Because this is a handbook, I've repeated some information that may have been cited elsewhere so that readers will not have to shuffle back and forth throughout the book. The question-and-answer format allows you to skip or skim sections you don't feel are relevant, although you are welcome to read the book straight through.

What I hope you will do is this: Order your own *free* copy of the NRP report at the panel's website, *www.nationalreadingpanel.org.* You will find the order form under the section marked "Documents" on the website. For each answer to questions that are relevant to your own classroom, I suggest you mark the report page with a sticky note, and highlight the quotation that I use to document my response to each question.

Keep the report on your desk to show parents, should they question your methods. Take the report to your principal and other school administrators to verify that the commercial programs being promoted by publishers, and even by the government, do not benefit children. In fact, you can show that such commercial programs can actually have a *negative* impact on reading performance.

Carry your highlighted copy of the report to school board meetings and read aloud from it, quoting its scientific results. The sight of the report alone—all five hundred pages of it—will help sway doubters in the audience. Take it with you everywhere. Sleep with it under your pillow. Science is on your side. Really.

I ordered the NRP from the website and received two separate books and a video. A friend of mine printed her copy directly off the website. How will I know how to find the information you present?

Finding our way around the NRP can be somewhat confusing, so first we'll look at the various formats of the NRP.

Parts of the NRP

- *The Summary Booklet:* This short, thirty-two-page booklet condenses the supporting data in the *Report of the Subgroups.* *The Summary Booklet* misreports the true findings of the panel. It is this brief, easy to read *Summary Booklet* as well as the continuing misrepresentation by some panel members that has led to the misinterpretations and misapplications of the actual findings of the NRP. In other words, the findings do not match the data in the actual report. In citing this booklet, I refer to it as *The Summary Booklet* followed with a page number: (*The Summary Booklet*, p. 5).
- The second source is the large *Report of the Subgroups,* the book containing over five hundred pages including data and tables. Each chapter in this section refers to one facet of reading that the panel attempted to analyze. The report in its entirety contains six chapters:

  Chapter 1, "Introduction and Methodology"
  Chapter 2, "Alphabetics" (Part 1, Phonemic Awareness; Part 2, Phonics)
  Chapter 3, "Fluency"
  Chapter 4, "Comprehension"
  Chapter 5, "Teacher Education and Reading Instruction"

Chapter 6, "Computer Technology and Reading Instruction"

In referencing these chapters, I list the chapter, followed by a hyphen and the page number. For example, "2-84" refers to Chapter 2, page 84 of the *Report of the Subgroups*. When citing parts of this report other than the six chapters, I will cite the report's title, followed by the page number: (*Report of the Subgroups*, p. 64).

- The third piece is a brief, fifteen-minute publicity video that praises the work of the panel and contains none of the limitations and qualifications of the lengthy *Report of the Subgroups*. I refer to it as *The NRP Video* when I cite it.

I also need to warn you, if you have an earlier version of the *Report of the Subgroups* printed off the panel's website, your page numbers will not match those I use here. The scientific National Reading Panel altered the first website version of the report without indicating that it had done so. If you couldn't wait to get your copy through the mail and printed it off the Internet soon after the NRP report was first posted, your page numbers will differ from those I provide here. If you have an *early* Internet version, as a general rule of thumb, subtract eight pages from the citations I list here. All page numbers I cite here match those in the free hard copy of the report because that is the version most of you will be working from.

There has always been so much controversy surrounding phonics instruction and now we have scientific research on phonics thrown into the equation. What is the role of phonics in teaching reading?

This question gets right to the heart of the matter. Instead of trying to answer it all at once, we need to look at it in segments. After all, phonics instruction for older children and for second-language learners is an entirely different matter than it is for younger children and for students whose first language is English.

But let's start with a general framework and see what the *Report of the National Reading Panel* tells us about the role of phonics in teaching reading.

THE NRP'S DEFINITION OF PHONICS

How does the NRP define "phonics" and what is the ultimate goal of phonics in reading instruction?

The NRP defines *phonics* in terms of its ultimate goal—application. What's important in this definition is that it does *not* describe phonics as decontextualized skill building, but in terms of *function*. I have emphasized the focus on application in the panel's definition of *phonics* as follows:

> Phonics instruction is a way of teaching reading that stresses the acquisition of letter-sound correspondences *and their use in reading and spelling*. The primary focus of phonics instruction is to help beginning readers understand how letters are linked to sounds (phonemes) to form letter-sound correspondences and *to help them learn how to apply this knowledge in their reading.* (*The Summary Booklet*, p. 8)

As the NRP reminds us, phonics is "a means to an end . . . In implementing systematic phonics instruction, educators must keep the *end* in mind and ensure that children understand the purpose of learning letter sounds and that they are able to apply these skills . . . in their daily reading and writing activities" (*The Summary Booklet*, p. 10). Phonics instruction that "focus(es) too much on the teaching of letter-sounds and not enough on putting them to use [is] unlikely to be effective" (p. 2-97). This is *extremely* important because it firmly defines phonics instruction in terms of authentic usage, thus precluding approaches and programs that focus on isolated skill and drill. I will provide more evidence from the NRP report to support the case against teaching phonics out of context as we proceed through the book.

TYPES OF PHONICS

What are the various approaches to teaching phonics that are identified by the NRP?

The National Reading Panel report makes the following distinctions among approaches to teaching phonics:

Analogy Phonics—Teaching students unfamiliar words by analogy to known words (e.g., recognizing that the rime segment of an unfamiliar word is identical to that of a familiar word, and then blending the known rime with the new word onset, such as reading *brick* by recognizing that *-ick* is contained in the known word *kick,* or reading *stump* by analogy to *jump.*

Analytic Phonics—Teaching students to analyze letter-sound relations in previously learned words to avoid pronouncing sounds in isolation.

Embedded Phonics—Teaching students phonics skills by embedding phonics instruction in text reading, a more implicit approach that relies to some extent on incidental learning.

Phonics Through Spelling—Teaching students to segment words into phonemes and to select letters for those phonemes (i.e., teaching students to spell words phonemically).

Synthetic Phonics—Teaching students explicitly to convert letters into sounds (phonemes) and then to blend the sounds to form recognizable words.[10]

We hear a lot about "systematic" phonics instruction as opposed to "incidental" phonics instruction. What's the difference?

The report states:

The hallmark of a *systematic* phonics approach or program is that a sequential set of phonics elements is delineated and these elements are taught along a dimension of explicitness depending on the type of phonics method employed. Conversely, with *incidental* phonics instruction, the teacher does not follow a planned sequence of phonics elements to guide instruction but highlights particular elements opportunistically when they appear in text. (*The Summary Booklet*, p. 8)

Is the distinction between systematic and incidental phonics an "either/or" choice? Can't I seize the "teachable moment" and still fulfill the district's pressures to teach phonics systematically?

Phonics instruction is not an "either/or" dichotomy. I always taught phonics "opportunistically" when a question arose as we were reading a Big Book or through a child's writing during writer's workshop. It is still possible to explicitly and systematically target sounds, and to document a child's individual instructional needs *without* resorting to isolated skill and drill. As we will see, the National Reading Panel leaves decisions about when, how, and even *if* phonics should be taught to the professional discretion of the teacher.

PANEL DID NOT IDENTIFY ONE BEST METHOD FOR PHONICS OR READING

Are you saying that the NRP doesn't identify any one "best" method of teaching phonics? I need to be able to justify my instruction to parents and school administrators. How can I do that?

I'm going to provide you with evidence here that the panel did *not* identify one best method for teaching phonics. More important, it clearly states in several places that there is no *one* "right" way to teach *reading!* You can use this research to establish that you must make the decisions in your own classroom. In an interview, the chair of the Alphabetics subcommittee, Linnea Ehri, "emphasized that the findings of the panel did not 'single out any one way to teach reading. Rather, multiple ways were found to be effective . . .' Thus the panel's results cannot be claimed to dictate any one method." Another comment in this interview is worthy of our notice: Ehri states, "teachers should not abandon whole language instruction."[11]

Another member of the National Reading Panel, S. J. Samuels, agrees with Ehri that no single method is better than any other.

> Many of our educational pundits appear to believe there are universal approaches to instruction and development of curricular materials which will work for all children under all conditions. They seem to ignore differences in intelligence and home background conditions. Depending on these variables as well as the degree of motivation and prior knowledge brought to the task of learning to read, it is highly likely that some approaches to instruction should be better for some children and different approaches should work better for other children.[12]

We will explore the role of the teacher in more depth as we look at the panel's recommendations on motivational factors and making effective instructional changes in classrooms. It's important, however, that you can first defend your right to structure your classroom according to methods suggested by your own expertise, rather than what outsiders dictate. Just remember, the chair of the Alphabetics subcommittee and the cochair of the Fluency subcommittee of the NRP report have determined that no single reading method was found to be better than another!

PANEL'S DEFINITION OF READING: DISCRETE SUBSKILLS

How did the NRP define reading? The definition of reading has an enormous impact on how it is assessed, doesn't it? Our standardized tests examine discrete subskills such as decoding and word identification, but as you stated, children can sometimes decode with accuracy and yet not comprehend.

Here we come to an important internal contradiction and research flaw in the NRP report. In order to explain it, we need to get into some research and statistical terminology. You can, if you wish, just skip this section and come back to it when you need it. Recall that the panel clearly defined *phonics* in terms of function and emphasizes that role throughout the report. However, the National Reading Panel did *not* provide a definition of *reading* as a process.

In a sense, it defined reading as isolated skills that could be mastered and performed by children regardless of whether or not they could actually apply the skills to text.

As proof, the report selected studies for what is termed a *meta-analysis*, an approach that allows researchers to analyze the outcomes of a number of studies in a given area and to identify a consistent result. Another way of putting it is that a meta-analysis is designed to synthesize the findings of a number of studies on a topic and come to a consensus. In the NRP report's section on phonics, the panel supposedly wanted to determine whether phonics instruction helped children's reading growth. Recall that one requirement of a meta-analysis is that the outcomes of the studies be conceptually consistent and must all assess outcomes, or *dependent variables*, that are conceptually similar. A meta-analysis cannot legitimately compare dissimilar concepts, find an average of each study result, and declare a common outcome. In other words, it cannot compare apples and billy goats and declare its findings to be a synthesis of *fruit*. However, what the panel did was to use studies with various and sundry outcomes that did not necessarily reflect what they defined as the ultimate goal of phonics instruction—application to authentic text. Already we see an inconsistency between what the panel said was important and what it actually measured.

One way to look at it is like this: The NRP performed a sort of research sleight of hand and attempted to circumvent the requirement for consistency by labeling *any* single isolated reading skill—or any combination of reading subskills—"General Reading" or "General Literacy." The problem with the panel's approach is obvious to real teachers. We all know that just because a child can, for example, decode phonetically regular words or even read fluently, such behavior does not necessarily guarantee comprehension. The ability to decode phonetically regular words on little lists is a different *concept* than comprehending a text or generating a fluid, logically organized, written piece. The isolated reading skills that the report's studies accepted as determining "reading growth" are divided into six separate and discrete subcategories:

- Decoding: This subcategory assessed the reading of words with regular spelling patterns in isolation—for example, *cat, fat, mat.*
- Pseudowords: This subcategory assessed children's ability to read pseudowords with regular spelling patterns—for example, *dat, wat, gat.*
- Word Identification: This subcategory assessed children's ability to read words in isolation. Some consisted of regular spelling patterns while others did not.
- Spelling: This subcategory assessed the children's ability to spell words. With the younger children, kindergartners and first graders, invented spelling was accepted—for example *fet* for *feet* and *kr* for *car*. For older children (grades 2 through 6) only conventional spelling was accepted.
- Oral Reading: The panel did not provide a definition for oral reading.
- Comprehension: For younger children, this usually involved "extremely short (usually one-sentence) 'passages' ". Often these tests favored "phonetically regular words." For older children, the tests were usually passages from standardized tests or tests developed for training purposes by the researchers (2-115). The distinction between the types of assessments used for younger and older children is extremely important when we look at the impact of phonics on comprehension.
- General Reading or General Literacy: The effect sizes (here it helps to think "results") for each subcategory listed above were combined for each of the thirty-eight studies to produce an averaged effect size. The panel claimed that this averaged effect size for each study represented children's reading growth. The panel then combined all the averaged effect sizes for each set of comparisons in the studies and averaged them. This final, averaged outcome for the individual comparisons was named General Literacy.

Here now is the sleight of hand. The panel averaged these single, isolated comparisons and instead of naming this averaged outcome *skills* or growth *in isolated skills*, they named it General Reading—a misnomer!

Any one study in the analysis could look at from one to six of the subcategories listed above, but most looked at only two or three comparisons. Some studies actually assessed only one subcategory and yet the results were still termed "Reading." No study tested for all six subcategories, and the majority focused on single words rather than comprehension.[13] In spite of the panel's assertion that phonics must result in application to authentic literacy activities, only 24 percent of the studies *even involved text!* Of that 24 percent, only 16 percent of the studies the panel used actually looked at comprehension (2-111). You can see the statistical research alchemy here. It would be wonderful if competence in isolated reading subskills guaranteed transfer to comprehension, but we all know that it is just not so. As we will see later in our discussion, the panel's own meta-analysis clearly demonstrates that such skills, taught essentially in isolation as they were, did *not* transfer to authentic text or even to conventional spelling, much less to writing.

The effect sizes (here it helps to think "results") for each subcategory (as listed above) was measured in what is termed *standard deviation units*. The mean (think *averaged result*) for each of the subcategories in each study was calculated and expressed as 0. An effect size of 0, therefore, indicates that there was no statistically significant difference between the results for the treatment and control groups—the training had no effect because both groups did the same. An effect size of 1.0 indicated that the treatment group mean was one standard deviation unit higher than the control group mean. The panel decided that an effect size of 0.20 is *small*; an effect size of 0.50 is *moderate* and an effect size of 0.80 is *large* (2-112). For a more detailed description of the statistical procedures the panel used, see "Coding of Data" (*The Summary Booklet*, pp. 29–33). You can refer back to this section on what is *small*, *moderate* and *large* in terms of results when we come to the actual findings.

NRP'S CAUTION AGAINST OVERLY STRESSING PHONICS AND THE NEED FOR BALANCE

As you say, there is enormous pressure to stress phonics in reading instruction at all grade levels. What does the scientific research tell us about the appropriate role of phonics in teaching reading? I have the impression from all the publicity surrounding the NRP report that phonics should be the dominant focus of instruction. Is this true?

We've all seen the headlines claiming that the NRP urges intensive, systematic phonics instruction for all children in grades K–6. However, what we don't see in the headlines or in the promotional ads for commercial programs is that the NRP stresses phonics instruction as part of a "balanced reading program." The report states that teachers must *not* "allow phonics to become the dominant component not only in the time devoted to it, but also in the significance attached. It is important *not* to judge children's reading competence solely on the basis of their phonics skills." (*The Summary Booklet*, p. 11). We can use this information from the report to defend our classrooms against pressures and programs that emphasize phonics too heavily. And what qualifies as "too heavy" an emphasis? *You* are the teacher. *You* decide. Remember, the chair of the Alphabetics subcommittee of the report said there *is* no single best method to teach reading. As we will see, the National Reading Panel emphasizes throughout its report that the role of the teacher cannot be underestimated.

I hear a lot about "balanced reading instruction." What is meant by the term balance?

The NRP clearly states that teachers must emphasize interesting, engaging books and that they should not place so much focus on phonics skills that children lose sight of the ultimate goal of reading. We must not, declares the NRP, "devalue their [children's] interest in books because they cannot decode with complete accuracy" (*The Summary Booklet*, p. 11).

Thus, we can use the science of the NRP to defend our efforts to keep "real reading" from becoming subordinate to phonics. Furthermore, providing balance through a focus on lots of opportunities for immersion in print actually helps students acquire skills. The NRP report notes that, "quality literature helps students to build a sense of story and to develop vocabulary and comprehension." In providing a balanced program, the active engagement and motivation of students and teachers is a key element. Thus the report warns us to avoid "'dull drill' and 'meaningless worksheets' "(2-97). In other words, the NRP cautions that too heavy an emphasis on isolated phonics ignores "motivational factors . . . 'relevance' and 'interest value' " (2-96). Balance, then, means using lots of literature to teach skills *such as phonics* within meaningful, motivating contexts that demonstrate how such skills are actually applied.

The chairman of the National Reading Panel, Donald N. Langenberg, Ph. D., reminds us that "Reading is an enormously complex activity" (*The NRP Video*). Therefore, it's a mistake to try to oversimplify it by focusing too much on phonics. The NRP report states, "By emphasizing *all* of the processes that contribute to growth in reading, teachers will have the best chance of making every child a reader" (2-97).

What can we do to make sure that all the processes mentioned by the NRP report are included in the curriculum?

Panel member Joanna P. Williams indicates that traditionally, comprehension has been neglected. She states, "We have had a lot of work in beginning reading on phonics . . . but we haven't done too much on comprehension" (*The NRP Video*). If we accept Williams' statement, we can surmise that perhaps because we have focused too much on the isolated bits and pieces at the expense of comprehension, many children have been left behind and are confused about the actual purpose of reading—understanding!

NRP'S SUPPORT FOR INVESTING IN CLASSROOM LIBRARIES (ASSISTANT SECRETARY OF EDUCATION SUSAN NEUMAN'S RESEARCH)

What does the NRP say we should do to improve comprehension instruction?

This question takes us back to the report's emphasis on balancing skills by teaching them through quality literature. The NRP's instructional video recommends "active involvement between reader and the text . . . .Student achievement is linked to children's ability to understand and enjoy what they read." For such active engagement to occur, the NRP states that teachers must be sure to include "quality literature that helps students to build a sense of story and to develop vocabulary and comprehension" (2-97).

In order to balance instruction as the NRP suggests, there must be funding for books. My classroom library is small and was built with books that I purchased myself. Our school library is small and I know of schools that actually have no library. I need specific evidence to bring to our school board to support using school money to acquire books.

How sad that teachers must actually justify purchasing books as if allowing children to read were some covert activity calculated to rob us of time and money for phonics. But help is on the way to back the purchase of books *and* class time for "real" reading. You can bolster the NRP's conclusion that instruction must be balanced by using the words of George W. Bush's assistant secretary of education, Susan Neuman. Her own research, coauthored with Donna Celano, emphasizes the importance of environmental factors on children's cognitive and social development. I'm including several quotes taken directly from a speech she made at a White House educational summit. Titled "Access to Print: Problem, Consequences, and Day One Instructional Solutions," Neuman's speech offers overwhelming evidence that children must be immersed in print in order to become good readers as well as to help them acquire skills such as those we measure on standardized tests.[14]

The Neuman-Celano study compared the totality of print environments in poor and middle-class neighborhoods. It counted the number of bookstores, books, signs, types of signs, and opportunities for children to see *others* reading, as well as the number of libraries. The "goal was to examine the neighborhood from the perspective of a young child learning about print, the amount and types of text, exposures to reading."[15] The differences were startling. The middle-class children were surrounded by a variety of reading materials. Even the signs in middle-class neighborhoods were bright and well kept. In contrast, the children from less affluent environments were in many respects print deprived and have access to far fewer bookstores, libraries, and well-lit places to read. Even the signs in poorer neighborhoods were less welcoming, often consisting of graffiti carrying threatening messages. Thus, print for children in such environments can actually carry *negative* connotations.

NEED FOR PRINT IMMERSION
TO FACILITATE SKILLS ACQUISITION

What was the ultimate impact of print immersion as opposed to print deprivation?

Neuman states:

> The results impacted all aspects of children's development. Children in high-print areas, where they have been nourished with print from the very beginning, are likely to read at their instructional level, whereas low-income children are likely to read below their level. We referred to it simply as "reading up"— or challenging material; and "reading down"—reading low level materials. Before technology came into the library, what we note is a gap. Children in high-print communities spend more time reading and engaged in literacy related activity. They spend less time milling around. In contrast, kids in low-print environments spend less time reading, less time in literacy related activity, and more time milling around. The bigger concern is that with new

technologies, the gap dramatically increases. Reading increases more for high-print communities than low-print, and milling around and not much (using the space at the library but not for its original purpose) is dramatically increasing. Examining computer activities in particular, we find that children from high-print communities read more lines of print, spend more minutes on applications, and more time on the computer. Further, they spend more time on challenging materials than those from low-print areas. Thus the "digital divide" is really a "literacy divide."[16]

The bottom line, Neuman concludes, is that children who are exposed to print read more, and "read up." That is, they select more challenging materials. Children who have had *less* exposure to print read less, and "read down"—they read less challenging material. Now remember, this study did not look at direct instruction of skills. All it assessed was the impact of lots of print on how children read, how *much* they read, *and* as we are about to see, the kinds of reading skills they acquired just by being surrounded by print. Thus, we have excellent support from "their" own research for purchasing books for our classrooms.

Our district is very focused on test results. Many of those results are based on children's performance on isolated skills such as those we saw in the NRP report. I need to justify expenditures for books based on potentially higher test scores. For many, it is those scores—based on skills—that are the bottom line. I am accountable to an army of people—parents, school administrators, and other teachers who criticize my literature-based classroom as being cognitively "soft." I need a solid, research-based answer for these critics.

Again, you can cite George W. Bush's assistant secretary of education. Susan Neuman's research clearly establishes that the acquisition of basic reading skills is strongly dependent on children's exposure to books and literature:

> The first ramification has been made famous by Keith Stanovich and is called the "environmental opportunity hypothesis." Here, limited exposure to print is considered a major factor since children will not likely hear the phonology of print—the

sounds of words. For Keith Stanovich, phonological coding or phonemic awareness is at the heart of learning to read. When children are not exposed to the sounds of our language, they have difficulty learning to connect sounds and symbols. With this difficulty, they are likely to have difficulty identifying words, then reading words with fluency. With slow decoding of words, they are easily frustrated, and thus begins a cycle of discouraging efforts, with children shying away from print. On the other hand, those children who have had lots of experience hearing similarities and differences in sounds are likely to grasp the alphabetic principle, start identifying words rather easily, enjoy it and thus begins a cycle of motivation and reading. . . . Limited access to books will unfortunately lead to limited vocabulary (since vocabulary development and rare word acquisition is related to print experiences) and limited information. . . . Less information will mean slower schema developing. (We know, for example, that knowledge leads to more knowledge, since we have organization schema on which to connect new ideas.) (Neuman 2001)

This documented, well-researched cycle of success increasing the chance for success—and of failure breeding more failure—has been called the "Matthew Effect" ("the rich get richer and the poor get poorer"), after the Gospel according to St. Matthew. Again, powerful support for providing lots of books and time for real reading comes from the assistant secretary of education. You can state that basic skills such as those assessed on standardized tests are acquired through lots of reading by quoting Susan Neuman as she cites the classic work of the well-respected scientific researcher, Keith Stanovich.[17]

NRP RESEARCH SUPPORTING SSR

Our district wants to eliminate sustained silent reading (SSR) because it takes too much time from direct instruction. Furthermore, our administrators are claiming that the NRP does not support SSR. I need research support for keeping, not just books, but time for the reading of books in my classroom.

First, the NRP report does NOT say that sustained silent reading is ineffective. Here is an important quote from the report that you can cite:

> There has been widespread agreement in the literature that encouraging students to engage in wide, independent, silent reading increases reading achievement. Literally hundreds of correlational studies find that the best readers read the most and that poor readers read the least. These correlational studies suggest that the more that children read, the better their fluency, vocabulary and comprehension. (*The Summary Booklet*, p. 12)

We will recall here that the panel claimed it only included experimental studies. In point of fact, the NRP could not find enough of experimental studies to conduct a meta-analysis in its subgroup report on "Comprehension." Furthermore, the studies it did include in its analysis of "comprehension," "varied widely in their methodological quality and the reading outcome variables measured" (*The Summary Booklet*, p. 12). In other words, the NRP did not have enough studies of reasonable, consistent quality to draw a firm, "scientific" conclusion.[18] The report states, "No doubt, it could be that the more that children read, the more their reading skills improve, but it is also possible that better readers simply choose to read more" (*The Summary Booklet*, p. 12).

Second, we have powerful defense for devoting class time to sustained silent reading. James Cunningham, a highly respected quantitative researcher, reviewed the NRP report. That review is published in *Reading Research Quarterly*, the publication that Assistant Secretary of Education Susan Neuman states is "the highest quality journal in the field."[19] In Cunningham's scientific analysis of the NRP report, he documents that the panel's claim of using only the medical model for determining its findings was not consistently applied throughout and within the various chapters (subgroups) in the report. Cunningham states, "Members of the Comprehension Subgroup [the section examining SSR] found few studies that met the NRP criteria and did not perform any meta-analyses, but they chose to summarize the research they examined and make instructional recommendations anyway. . . ."[20]

In other words, *even if* we accept the premise that the medical model can appropriately inform us about the complexities of the reading process, the panel didn't apply its own scientific criteria when it made its determination about direct comprehension instruction or sustained silent reading. Furthermore, according to Cunningham, the panel's recommendations reflect its own subjective determinations and biases. Based on nonscientific research, the panel nonetheless determined that direct, explicit instruction benefits comprehension. On the other hand, it rejected the "literally hundreds" of correlational studies showing, in the chapter on "Fluency," that SSR improved children's reading skills claiming that *those* studies were *not* scientific. Cunningham states:

> There is a definite downside, however, to the panel's willingness to make instructional recommendations for comprehension based on looser criteria than it was willing to follow in the alphabetics and fluency sections. For example, members are willing to endorse text comprehension instruction but not interventions to increase independent silent reading, even though neither type of instruction met their original specifications for classroom implementation. Doesn't this reveal a bias toward explicit instruction rather than just a scientific finding of its superiority? Doesn't this suggest that the panel thinks word identification and oral reading are more important, and therefore more deserving of scientific, objective, and rigorous research standards than comprehension and independent silent reading?[21]

We have even more scientific evidence to support SSR and again, we can refer to the scientific research of George W. Bush's own assistant secretary of education. The NRP report was released well before Susan Neuman's scientific study emphasizing the impact of a literate, book-rich reading environment on children's cognitive development and, therefore, could not be included in the report. Neuman emphasizes the importance of immersing children in reading and surrounding them not only with books but with *readers*. Her research concludes, "Environment has a powerful effect. As Bruner suggested and perhaps said it best, 'place people in a library and they act like they're in the library, put people on the ball field, and they play ball.' "[22] We can reasonably conclude, as

Neuman does, that if we surround children with books and lots of readers, they will read!

SCIENTIFIC RESEARCH SUPPORTING LITERATURE AND CONTEXTUALIZED INSTRUCTION (NEUMAN'S RESEARCH)

We are being pressured to heavily gear our classrooms toward explicit, direct instruction, much of it at the expense of more authentic, literature-based activities. My experience has taught me that children learn when tasks are authentic and they actually experience the connection between activities and real-life application. What does the science tell us about contextualized, meaningful instruction?

We have seen from James Cunningham's analysis of the NRP report that its recommendation for explicit, direct instruction was *not* based on the panel's own medical-model criteria for research. But we have yet more evidence to defend our belief we must teach skills in context. You can support building a literate classroom community based on authentic, contextualized instruction by citing Neuman's own government-sponsored research. Susan Neuman offers the following conclusions about how our classrooms should be focused:

> Changes in designs of classrooms are needed and important; however, they cannot begin to bridge the gulf between school learning and the more informal learning that occurs in daily activity. A second and more dramatic accommodation is to broaden our definitions of literacy from one that is school bound to one that is more situation based. Strategies for learning about literacy need to be tied to the more context-based problems and techniques of practical life. A better balance between decontextualized learning and functional activity might take advantage of what children bring to the school setting focusing on a wider range of capabilities rather than perceived incapabilities and deficiencies.[23]

Furthermore, Neuman's scientific research emphasizes that children must be engaged in meaningful *play* as well as work. She states,

"Much of the work on literacy and play has been to create contexts that engage young children in problem solving activity, reflecting the types, uses of literacy and scripts and routines in everyday life."[24] Neuman recognizes the importance of surrounding children with books and of giving them time to become comfortable and at ease with them. She cites the "familiarity hypothesis" derived from Michael Cole and Sylvia Scribner's classic study of the Vai people in Africa. Neuman concludes that the research clearly shows:

> Those children who are familiar with activities develop cognitive routines associated with them. They know how stories work and are likely to predict what comes next. They develop the mental models that go with different types of texts; and familiarity breeds contentment, and comfort.[25]

In other words, if we want children to be readers, they must perceive themselves as readers. For that to happen, we must surround them with books, let them see others reading, and allow them lots of time to read themselves. Again, you are not citing Elaine Garan here. This comes directly from George W. Bush's assistant secretary of education.

RESEARCH SUPPORTING PARENTAL SUPPORT

What I understand from the scientific research supporting the need for literate, book-rich environments is that for optimum success, the environment must extend beyond the school. How important is parental involvement?

You can cite panel member Joanne Yatvin to focus attention on the need for family involvement. Like Neuman, she emphasizes the vital need for "home support for literacy" as "experts believe they are critical determinants of school success or failure" (p. 2).[26] In addition to Yatvin, Susan Neuman supports the importance of family involvement as a result of research findings based on a government-funded grant. The study determined that schools must change the relationships among teachers, administrators, and families and that we must advocate more funding for family libraries and book clubs:

> Yet, there is no way that we can be successful without parent involvement and parent education. In Philadelphia we were able to use a grant from the Barbara Bush Foundation to develop a highly successful family literacy project. We established book clubs and helped parents understand how books are used for literacy development in prekindergarten and kindergarten classrooms. We then encouraged parents to read with their child (using the language they felt most comfortable with) at school using a variety of genre from predictable books to narratives. Language and literacy skills [were] within three months significantly enhanced far more [than] what the teacher alone could do. We were so successful that parents continued the book clubs after we were gone. This particular parent in the slide [shown to the audience] actually became an aide to a librarian. Thus it is critical at this exciting time that we begin to recognize that enhancing children's cognitive development can work together with enhancing their social emotional development—that we in education must work together to move away from ideological stances to what works for children.[27]

Notice Neuman doesn't mention direct instruction or teaching phonemes or giving parents flashcards to work with their children. Her message is very clear: surround children with books, read with them, and give them time to read on their own.

You've relied very heavily on Susan Neuman's work. Why? Isn't there research beyond what she and the NRP have conducted to support the importance of immersion in print, authentic, contextualized instruction, and family literacy?

Yes, there is. But what I am providing here is scientific research that is irrefutable on the government's own scientific ground. Neuman is a highly respected researcher. She is the assistant secretary of education in the Bush administration *and* her work is government funded. These are arguments that make her findings extremely powerful. The government or your school district cannot very easily refute the findings of the study sponsored by the

Barbara Bush Foundation, especially when the research was completed by the assistant secretary of education. Remember, we are blinding them with their *own* science. And quite legitimately!

What is the most effective way to ensure the recommended balance between skills and authentic application?

The results of the NRP report fully support Neuman's findings that skills are acquired through authentic literacy activities. The data from the NRP report clearly demonstrate that decontextualized skills taught in isolation do *not* transfer to authentic literacy activities such as comprehension and spelling. Given the base we have established for print-rich environments, I think it is appropriate at this juncture to look at the NRP results for commercial programs because they represent the antithesis of the recommendations of the NRP and the assistant secretary of education.

COMMERCIAL PHONICS PROGRAMS AND THE PANEL'S WARNINGS AGAINST THEIR USE

In reviewing commercial phonics programs, we've noticed a rigidity in terms of instruction. Programs such as Open Court and Direct Instruction don't seem to allow for individual differences in students. Does "one size fit all"?

The NRP agrees with your observation that commercial programs fail to meet either the instructional or the motivational needs of children and teachers. Perhaps because teachers and schools are so open to public scrutiny and are so vulnerable to criticism, quick-fix cure-alls can appear very attractive at first. Sometimes it is easy for us as teachers—as well as for the public—to forget the enormous amounts of money that publishers make on schools. It's easy to succumb to the allure of the slickly pitched, flawlessly presented programs because they *promise* us results. It's also easy to forget that the publishers of commercial programs are focused on their own bottom line—profit—rather than the needs of our children. Anyone who's taught for a period of time has seen the way the "philosophies" of publishers shift with the prevailing swing of the pendulum. When whole language was "in," basals and even phonics programs had the term *whole language* plastered on their covers.

Now that phonics is back, publishers have dusted off their old wares, put flashy new covers on them, and resurrected them. Thus we see the old DISTAR program now repackaged as Direct Instruction or Reading Mastery while Open Court, which has been used *and* rejected by schools for *years*, is now experiencing a second or a third or fifth or tenth coming. You can use the fact that these programs are *nothing new*. As we review the history of these new-old commercial programs, a question arises: "If they were so wonderful, why were they adopted and eventually rejected by schools in the first place?" Doesn't it make sense that since they have been around for years, and if they were truly successful, then every school in the country would be using them by now without being pressured by the government to do so?

Here is a warning against the use of commercial programs by panel member Timothy Shanahan, who cautions us that "schools are barraged with commercial products and gurus who come through with some new product or magic cure for children's reading needs" and states that we must stop looking for "the magic bullet."[28]

In spite of commercial publishers' claims, we can find yet more support in the *Report of the National Reading Panel* for keeping commercial programs such as DISTAR and Open Court out of our classrooms. The NRP notes that commercial phonics programs are inflexible and ignore children's individual, developmental needs. Programs such as Open Court are heavily scripted and fail to allow for children's diverse backgrounds, learning styles, and needs. The NRP clearly cautions against such blanket, one-size-fits-all phonics instruction: "At all grade levels, but particularly in kindergarten and the early grades, children are known to vary greatly in the skills they bring to school" (*The Summary Booklet,* p. 11). "However," cautions the NRP, "it is common for many phonics programs to present a fixed sequence of lessons scheduled from the beginning to the end of the school year" (2-97). If you are underlining quotations from this book, don't neglect to use this one.

We can infer from the report that commercial programs not only put too much emphasis on phonics but also ignore the individual needs of students. The NRP asks the question, "Does one size fit all?" The NRP's answer is absolutely not! (2-95).[29] Do commercial programs such as Open Court and Direct Instruction impose rigid, inflexible, fixed sequences of instruction that *directly contradict* the recommendations of the NRP? Yes, of course they do! So we can *use* the NRP's science to protect our children from commercial programs.

OPEN COURT

I "test drove" Open Court and found myself nodding off as I was teaching. The program was that boring! It was hard for me to remain engaged in the rote, boring drills. Is this an unusual reaction to scripted programs?

Absolutely not! The NRP clearly states that teaching is a process in which both the students and the teacher must be actively engaged and motivated. If we want to apply the scientific research of the NRP to commercial programs, we cannot ignore the role of motivation for teachers as well as students. The National Reading Panel emphasizes throughout its report that the role of the teacher cannot be underestimated. Some commercial programs, states the NRP, "are scripted in such a way that teacher judgment is largely eliminated. Although scripts may standardize instruction, they may reduce teachers' interest in the teaching process" (2-96). The report states that scripted phonics programs may interfere not only with the learner's motivation, but also with the teacher's motivation. The NRP states, "It seems self-evident that teachers will be most effective when they are enthusiastic in their teaching and enjoy what they are doing in their classroom" (2-7). The report continues:

> The lack of attention to motivational factors by researchers in the design of phonics programs is potentially very serious because debates about reading instruction often boil down to concern about the "relevance" and "interest value" of *how* something

is being taught, rather than the specific content of *what* is being taught. (2-97)

We can bolster the power of the previous statement by the NRP on the importance of motivation by referring to Susan Neuman's scientific research: "For too many of our children, instruction fails to 'engage their minds.' Children's minds atrophy with limited stimuli."[30]

Let me pose a question. When you are following a rigid script, are you enthusiastic about your role as a teacher? If we follow the advice of the "coaches" and try to instill excitement into drills that are regimented, dull, and boring, are we being truly honest with children? I know that I did not become a teacher to mindlessly train children to mindlessly perform. The teachers I remember with warmth and appreciation were not automatons who dispensed worksheets. They were the creative, innovative teachers who honored my uniqueness, even my quirks, and got me hooked on learning, not on phonics. I hope that my legacy to my students will be the same. It's worth thinking about. Scientific research supports active learning.

But how can I convince administrators and even parents that Open Court and other commercial programs are ineffective?

First, as we have seen, you can cite from the NRP report about motivation and about the need for individualizing instruction. You can also cite Linnea Ehri, chair of the Alphabetics subcommittee of the NRP report, and S. J. Samuels, cochair of the Fluency subcommittee. Remember, they both said that there is NO ONE BEST METHOD FOR TEACHING READING (see p. 12–13). Second, invite any doubters into your classroom to actually participate in Open Court or Direct Instruction. Request that they sit in, not for just a few minutes, and not for just one morning of rote instruction, but for an entire week so that they can get the full impact of the program. Tell them that at the end of that period you will administer the same tests that we are required to give to children, just to make sure they are paying attention. I seriously doubt that a single adult could endure what we require of children.

If boring doubters into recognizing the folly of commercial programs is ineffective, rest assured we can convince them with
irrefutable data demonstrating that such programs are actually
worse than nothing. The section that follows provides you with
data showing that commercial phonics programs actually have a
negative impact on children's comprehension and spelling.

*Wait a minute. The sales representatives for commercial
programs such as Open Court and Direct Instruction claim that
"scientific research" proves the effectiveness of their programs.
If we apply the NRP's criteria for effective phonics instruction
to commercial programs, they are actually incompatible with
what the NRP recommends. What's going on here?*

What's going on here is that we are being presented with a skill-
ful, insidious sales pitch that is hard to counter because the basis
of the campaign is "research" and "science," two concepts that
many of us don't have the background to argue against. Furthermore, the science that some publishing companies are pandering
appears to have the sanction of the government behind it.

*So are you saying that research does NOT support the use of
commercial programs such as Open Court and Direct
Instruction?*

That is *exactly* what I am saying. Furthermore, it is not just my
opinion. Research data show that not only are commercial programs such as Open Court and Direct Instruction *not* effective,
but actually have a *negative* impact on children's reading.

*What is the "proof" for that statement? How can we prove it
to our school boards, parents, and administrators?*

First, the National Reading Panel itself emphasized that phonics
is a means to an end, a tool, the ultimate goal of which is application to authentic reading and writing activities. Having reaffirmed

this basic belief, let us now look at the NRP's research for commercial programs, starting with Open Court.

THE RESULTS FOR OPEN COURT

Here we need a brief review of some basic research terms. In research terminology, what most of us would refer to as "results" or "outcomes" are termed *effect sizes*. Statisticians make arbitrary decisions. An effect size of 0.20 is considered to be small or "weak," while 0.50 is "moderate" and 0.80 is arbitrarily considered to be "large." Keeping that in mind, let us look at the outcomes, or effect sizes, for the research on Open Court in the NRP report.

If you wish to cross-check the results I list here, you can turn to Appendix G in the NRP *Report of the Subgroups*. The studies are listed according to the researcher(s)/author(s) and are assigned a number. I have provided Appendix G from the NRP report in Appendix A of this book. The numbered list of the studies alone is in Appendix B of this book. For ease of referencing, the studies are assigned the same numbers here as are used in the NRP report. The numbers precede the actual citations for the each study. The NRP report includes one study that examined the impact of Open Court on first and second graders after one year of intensive training.[31] The children were put into two groups. The group that received no training was called the "control group" while the group that was trained using Open Court was called the "treatment group."

First Grade: The Outcomes for Open Court (Study No. 11)

Decoding for first grade. In the Foorman study (#11) at the end of the school year, the first graders were administered posttests that required them to decode phonetically regular words. Not surprisingly, children's ability to decode was high (1.14) perhaps because the words were regularly patterned. The list used in the assessment contained no surprises and none of the irregularities such as those that children must negotiate in authentic reading.

Spelling for first grade. The category Spelling accepted invented spellings such as *fet* for *feet* or *cr* for *car*. Even though children were *not* required to spell conventionally, the effect size was still barely moderate (0.56).

Comprehension for first grade. For Comprehension the results were "small" (0.32) even though the passages were brief and consisted primarily of phonetically regular, easily decodable words.

Well, don't those results show that Open Court is actually pretty effective? After all, Open Court still showed positive results for decoding, spelling, and comprehension, right?

Ah, now we will see what is really going on here. The Open Court results for first grade—while not great—are so-so, at least on isolated skills and easily decoded, short, "comprehension" passages. We need to remind ourselves that even "so-so" outcomes are the result of an enormous investment in terms of time, motivation, and money. Would your district be satisfied to make such an enormous expenditure to achieve only small and moderate results? Now see what happens when children are required to apply Open Court phonics to authentic text.

Second Grade: The Outcomes for Open Court (Study No. 11)

We need to keep in mind that the assessments differ for children at various grade levels. For kindergartners and first graders, the assessments were short and relied on easily decodable words or pseudowords and short, phonetically regular passages (2-115). Past first grade, children were required to apply the isolated learned phonics "rules" to texts that more accurately approximate real-life reading, writing, and spelling. What we see is a precipitous drop. Remember, this is the famous Foorman study that is setting educational policy and determining which texts teachers will use.

Decoding for second grade. Decoding shows a *huge* drop from the high 1.14 that we saw for first grade to a small 0.32. Decoding, even at higher grade levels, requires children to read only words in isolation that are phonetically regular in spelling! But what we really need to sit up and pay attention to are the outcomes for spelling and comprehension.

Spelling for second grade. Spelling drops from the moderate results we saw for first grade (0.56) to a NEGATIVE .019 (–0.19)! This is a *drop* of 0.75 when children are required to apply phonics to conventionally spelled words. What's worse, in comprehension the negative outcomes mean that the Open Court children, trained *extensively* using the program, did far *worse* than the children in the other group, the so-called control group who were taught by whole language. Study No. 11 in Appendix G (Appendix A in this book) confirms that this is *not* my interpretation, but is the honest, accurate reporting of the data.

Comprehension for second grade. Recall that for first grade, comprehension was a small of 0.32. For second grade, we see a drastic drop as the small effect size of 0.32 falls precipitously to NEGATIVE 0.19 (–0.19). Again, when children actually need to apply Open Court phonics to more authentic text and to actually *comprehend* what they read, they *can't do it!*

The research data on Open Court shows that after one year of intensive, expensive highly focused training, the children in the Open Court program did significantly *worse* on tasks requiring authentic application of skills for spelling and comprehension than those children who received *no* training at all. Consider the cost of Open Court in terms of money and time. Consider the motivational factors, the boring, routine skill and drill—and for what? For NEGATIVE results! This is worse than "money for nothing." It is money for *less* than nothing.[32]

That explains what happens with Open Court. But what about other commercial phonics programs?

The NRP looked at seven commercial phonics programs and the results were consistent. The primary difference in the outcomes were the result of which reading subskills the studies assessed. In other words, many of the studies did not assess comprehension or spelling or even oral reading, but focused solely on isolated skills, such as the decoding of phonetically regular words or the sounding out of pseudowords. As with Open Court, the outcomes for these programs dropped dramatically with the level of application to authentic literary tasks required of the children.

The following descriptions of the results (or outcomes) for commercial programs serve two purposes here. First, they may be relevant to you if your district is considering adopting a specific program and you need to address the "research" claims of the publishers. Second, they make a *powerful* statement about phonics instruction. That is, while the programs I cite from the NRP report differ in some of the particulars of instruction, they all have two things in common. First, they teach isolated skills and exclude their application to authentic, connected text. Second, we see a lack of transfer. Consistently, the children appear to compartmentalize their instruction. While they can regurgitate the skills exactly as they are taught and practiced, those skills are rigid and fragmented in the children's minds.

As I looked across the results of the research that I provide here, I was reminded of my early days as a reading specialist. I can remember the exhilaration I felt as I trained children in isolated phonics skills and then tested them. The results on the assessments I administered, such as those we see as the predominant research in the NRP, showed that my students made "significant" gains. As a result, I truly believed that the intensive training I gave children in isolated phonics helped to make them better readers. It was only when I began to look beyond the neatly fragmented assessments I administered as part of my Title I program to the children's performance in their classrooms, that I saw the folly of my "success." Those skills did not transfer. You will see evidence of the same folly in the results that follow.

THE RESULTS FOR DIRECT INSTRUCTION (DISTAR)

There were five studies that looked at Direct Instruction but they varied in terms of which subskill outcomes were assessed. Some only looked at an isolated subskill such as oral reading or decoding and nonword reading. I fully acknowledge that isolated skills instruction impacts isolated skills application. But our interest here is in looking at what the NRP and our own common sense has determined is the ultimate goal of phonics instruction—the application to authentic text. So, let's look at the most comprehensive study on Direct Instruction in the NRP report.

Study No. 72 on Direct Instruction[33]

In Study No. 72, kindergarten children were trained in Direct Instruction for four years while first-grade children were trained for three years. At the end of that *extensive* training period, the group that started in kindergarten showed no statistically significant gain in spelling (0.16) and only a weak effect size in comprehension (0.28).

The children who were trained in Direct Instruction beginning in first grade and who were taught using the program for three years reflected the same trend we saw for Open Court. They showed a NEGATIVE effect size (–0.12) for spelling. For comprehension the results were not statistically different than 0 (0.11). Again, we see the expensive long-term training did not significantly transfer to authentic text.

JOLLY PHONICS

The Jolly Phonics program showed similar short-term effects on isolated skills. The NRP reports in Study No. 74 that at the end of training, the kindergartners trained in the program were tested and showed high, significant gains in isolated skills application such as reading phonetically regular pseudowords. However, a year later, the NRP states, "The Jolly Phonics group outperformed the control group in reading and spelling words but not in reading comprehension" (1-125). The information I provided here is quoted directly from the "Discussion" section of the NRP report. The data in the Table G contradict this finding and show a weak effect size of 0.31 for comprehension but a NEGATIVE effect size of –0.03 for nonword reading. Which of these conflicting data is in error is anyone's guess so I suggest you go with the information I cited from the "Discussion" section as it is consistent with the other findings for commercial programs and is therefore probably more reliable than the conflicting data in Table G.

ORTON-GILLINGHAM

There were three studies in the NRP that examined Orton-Gillingham, and as with the previously mentioned commercial programs, the results were dismal for application to authentic text.

Study No. 41 on Orton-Gillingham[34]

This is the only study assessing Orton-Gillingham that showed any positive effect sizes for children in comprehension and spelling. The effect sizes for that one study were high for decoding of isolated words (0.71) but showed a drop to a weak 0.23 for spelling. The categories for comprehension and nonword reading were only moderate, 0.62 and 0.61 respectively. As unimpressive as these effect sizes are, they are the only results for Orton-Gillingham that indicate any transfer of phonics skills to authentic text.

Study No. 13 on Orton-Gillingham

Study No. 13 did not assess comprehension as an outcome. What it did show though was that second- and third-grade students who were intensively trained for sixty minutes a day for an entire year using Orton-Gillingham showed a moderate increase (0.58) in their ability to decode isolated words. Yet again we see that they did not apply the phonics rules they were taught to spelling, for which the effect size did not significantly differ from

0, (0.05). Again, we need to remember that this study did *not* look at comprehension.

Study No. 47 on Orton-Gillingham

Study No. 47 showed even more dismal results than Study No. 13 for Orton-Gillingham and it *did* assess comprehension. After one year of training, third-grade children showed a small effect size for reading isolated words (0.31). However, the children were not able to transfer their ability to decode isolated words to comprehension. The effect size for comprehension was not significantly different from 0 (0.09). Even application to oral reading proved to be a problem and the results were a NEGATIVE 0.29 (–0.29). But watch what happens in the follow-up study. The low effect size of 0.31 for word identification drops to a NEGATIVE 0.19 (–0.19). And comprehension drops precipitously, dangerously, from a not significant 0.09 to a low, low NEGATIVE 0.81 (–0.81)! How sad these results are for these children, who wasted so many hours being skilled and drilled only to actually *lose* this ground!

NRP CRITERIA FOR EVALUATING COMMERCIAL PROGRAMS

But what does all of this mean in terms of evaluating commercial programs?

Let's put this all together now. We have seen by examining the actual words of the NRP that phonics should not be the dominant feature of any reading program and that we must focus on all the complexities of the reading process. We've also documented that we must engage children in good literature in order to motivate them and help them appreciate story structure. Furthermore, the NRP report clearly emphasizes that phonics is but a "means to an end," the ultimate goal of which is the application of authentic text. We are cautioned by the scientific research that commercial programs are rigid and scripted and diminish the motivation not only of students but of teachers. Furthermore, as we have seen, the NRP warns against the dangers of inflexible, one-size-fits-all instruction. Keeping these important research findings of the National Reading Panel in mind, here are the key questions we need to ask when evaluating phonics programs:

- Is so much time required in the use of a given program that there is little time for the use of *quality* literature to motivate children's interest and to help them acquire a sense of story?
- After the purchase of a commercial program, is there sufficient money to *purchase* interesting literature?
- Does phonics instruction focus on "dull drill" and "meaningless worksheets"?
- Is the program focused on isolated skills instead of relevant application of phonics to authentic reading and writing activities?
- Does the program rely so heavily on phonics that it makes phonics the dominant component in the reading program instead of a means to an end?
- Is the program scripted so that teacher judgment is eliminated?
- Does the program operate under the assumption that one size fits all and that all children should be taught the same skills at the same time?
- Is the program so routine and boring that students and teachers are not motivated?
- Does this program fail to honor my unique gifts as a teacher? Does it diminish my role as professional who knows and understands my students' needs?
- Does this program fail to honor the unique abilities, talents, and interests of my students?
- Do the results of the scientific research of the NRP show that children do not transfer isolated decoding skills to authentic text?

If the answer to even one of these questions is "yes" then the program is NOT scientifically based, according to the findings of the National Reading Panel. Isn't *that* a relief?

RESULTS FOR ISOLATED PHONICS INSTRUCTION

This all seems pretty obvious in terms of commercial programs, but what about noncommercial phonics instruction?

First, most of the studies in the NRP report's phonics section involved commercial programs. In fact, of the thirty-eight studies in this section, twenty-eight assessed commercial programs. Therefore, the results as I report them here are based largely on commercial programs. The panel did not distinguish between the results for commercial phonics programs and systematic phonics instruction as taught through other methods when it reported the final outcomes in its discussion section of the *Report of the Subgroups*, nor did it do so in *The Summary Booklet*. However, the pattern of nontransfer of isolated phonics instruction is absolutely consistent across the report. I have constructed a table (see page 43) showing the results of the panel's analysis. Remember, *these results are not my interpretation of the report.* They are taken *directly* from the panel's own data and their explanations in the discussion section.

As I look at this table, I don't see a category for "normal" readers or for ESL or for "high" readers. Why did the panel limit its analysis to "problem readers"?

We need to recall here that the panel limited the studies it included to those that used a medical model, assessing experimental methods on treatment and control groups. The majority of the studies that incorporate this model involved remediation approaches for children with reading difficulties. In terms of research protocols, the panel could not find enough studies with other groups of readers to include them in their conclusions. The panel divided its problem readers into two groups:

> *Younger Readers:* This group consisted of "at-risk" kindergarten and first graders (those who were at risk for developing reading problems).

Older Readers: This group consisted primarily of "disabled readers" (children with average or above-average intelligence who were not making normal progress in reading) and "low-achieving readers" ("children who were progressing poorly in reading and who varied in intelligence with at least some of them achieving poorly in other academic areas." (p. 2-82)

Limited English Proficiency students were excluded from the panel's analysis and there were too few normally achieving readers to draw conclusions about the impact of phonics on their reading growth. The omission of these categories of children means that the results *cannot* be applied to them.

Having noted the limitations of the study in terms of the students to which the findings can apply, I'm going to give you the bottom line first, followed by the evidence for that conclusion. Phonics had no statistically significant impact on tasks requiring authentic application. With the exception of a weak effect size for oral reading for older children the NRP's analysis shows that systematic phonics instruction resulted in significant outcomes *only* on those subcategories assessing phonetically regular words or words tested in isolation. For grades 2, 3, 4, 5, and 6, the grades at which the assessments required comprehension of more extended, authentic texts, phonics had no significant impact. Furthermore, the results for younger children (kindergartners and first graders) can only be applied to at-risk children.

What follows here are the reading subcategories that the panel used to determine reading. The outcomes (effect sizes) are taken directly from the discussion section of the *Report of the Subgroups*. Each subcategory is described in terms of the outcomes for younger children (children in kindergarten and first grade) and older children (children in second, third, fourth, fifth, and sixth grades). As you cross-check the following information with Table 1, note the drop in effect sizes as authentic text is introduced and also as we move from younger to older children. Note also that "older children" include any children above first grade!

TABLE 1 Results of the National Reading Panel's Analysis of Phonics Instruction

				Effect Sizes of the Subcategories			
	Decoding Words with regular spelling patterns only	*Pseudoword Reading* nonwords with regular spelling patterns only	*Word ID* Some words irregularly spelled	*Spelling*	*Oral Reading*	*Comprehension*	*General Reading* effect size of *all* categories
At-risk kindergaretn and 1st-grade students	0.98 high	0.67 mod.	0.45 small	0.67 mod. Accepted invented spellings	0.23 small based on 2 (K) and 4 (1st-gr.) studies**	0.51 mod. based on 1 (K) and 10 (1st-gr.) studies*	0.56 (K) and 0.54 (1st gr.) mod.
2nd–6th-grade disabled and low-achieving readers***	0.49 small to mod.	0.52 mod.	0.33 small	NO	0.24 small	NO	NO

Key:

NO = Not statistically significant. The individual effect sizes are not provided for results that were "not statistically significant" because the panel did not provide the outcomes for the "General Reading" outcome for "Older Readers." The results for that category were simply referred to as being not significant.

* The report states, "However, many of the studies were conducted with the beginning readers whose reading development at the time of the study was too limited to assess textual reading. We may question the use of the term "Comprehension" as it is applied to this group of at-risk, younger children.

** Results for K were BOTH NO. Two of the four effect sizes for first grade were NO. Results were based on two wildly heterogeneous outliers.

*** Indicates "There may have been too few studies in the database on low-achieving readers (eight) to draw firm conclusions."

EXPLANATION OF TABLE 1: RESULTS OF THE NRP'S ANALYSIS OF PHONICS INSTRUCTION

Decoding

Younger Children. The averaged effect size of decoding for kindergartners and first graders was 0.98 (high) and indicates that systematic phonics instruction does appear to help this population of at-risk children decode words, provided those words are phonetically regular and are tested in isolation.

Older Children. The average effect size of decoding for older low-achieving and reading disabled students was 0.49 (small to moderate) and indicates that systematic phonics instruction does appear to help problem readers to decode, provided the words are phonetically regular and are tested in isolation.

Reading of Pseudowords

Younger Children. The averaged effect size for pseudowords indicates a drop from the 0.98 for decoding to a moderate effect size of 0.67. It is reasonable to say that younger at-risk children may make moderate gains in decoding pseudowords, provided these words are phonetically regular and are tested in isolation. Perhaps the drop from decoding (in which at least some of the words were "real" words) indicates that the children relied at least to some extent on sight words and were not necessarily *decoding* all the words in that category.

Older Children. For older children, we notice that the effect size has dropped considerably from the moderate 0.67 that we saw for "younger children," to a moderate 0.52 for "older children." Thus, we see the beginning of a consistent trend as the impact of phonics instruction declines for older children. Recall that *all* of the pseudowords in this category are composed of phonetically regular spelling patterns and therefore should be easy to decode.

Word Identification

Younger Children. In this category, some words (we aren't told what percentage) having irregular spelling patterns are added to the outcome measures, so interestingly, the effect size drops from that of regularly patterned words (and pseudowords) to a small effect size of 0.45. However, the data do indicate that systematic phonics instruction does appear to help at-risk kindergarten and first-grade children to identify words, provided that the words are tested in isolation.

Older Children. Again we see a drop from the same category for younger children as the effect size falls from 0.45 (small) for younger children to an even weaker 0.33 for older children. The trend we see beginning here indicates that the results consistently decline as the children become older *and* as more authentic text is introduced. Even though the words in this category are tested in isolation, the introduction of even *some* words with irregular spelling patterns signals a decline in children's ability to perform the task. Notice the acceleration of the decline as we examine the outcomes for spelling and comprehension.

Spelling

There are no data indicating that systematic phonics significantly benefits children in spelling words conventionally at any grade level.

Younger Children. The subcategory of spelling for younger children accepted invented or developmental spellings. Even so, the findings indicate a only moderate averaged effect size of 0.67. However, there is no evidence to indicate if or how phonics instruction helps these at-risk children reconcile the regular spelling patterns emphasized in phonics programs with the vagaries of the English orthographic system. Therefore, in order to determine if phonics does, indeed, help children with conventional spelling, we must turn to averaged effect sizes for older children.

Older Children. The NRP report states, "The effect size for spelling (for children in 2nd through 6th grade) was not statistically different from zero (0.09) . . . [phonics was] not more effective than other forms of instruction in producing growth in spelling" (2-108). The panel offers an explanation for the nonsignificant effect size for spelling. The NRP report states that, "as readers move up in the grades, remembering the spellings of words is less a matter of applying letter-sound correspondences and more a matter of knowing more advanced patterns and morphologically based regularities which is not typically addressed in phonics instruction" (2-108).

Oral Reading

Younger Children. The averaged effect size for oral reading is weak, 0.23. However, it is highly questionable that even this weak outcome is accurate. As noted previously, the panel combined at-risk kindergartners and first graders. The results for oral reading were based on only two kindergarten and four first-grade studies. However, the effect sizes for the two kindergarten studies were both not significant (0.13 and 0.15), a fact that the panel does not mention in the discussion section of its report or in *The Summary Booklet.* I found this by examining Table G in the *Report of the Subgroups.* Furthermore, two of the four oral reading effect sizes for first grade were not significant (0 and 0.03). Remember, we are dealing with only six studies. Of these six studies, two kindergarten and two first-grade studies were *not* statistically significant. In other words, the four studies that were not significant were impacted by the only two studies in the set that were significant. Those two studies both had unusually high effect sizes and appear to be large outliers (8.79 and 2.18). Based on so few studies with such uneven results, the oral reading outcome for younger students (0.23, weak) cannot be a legitimate finding.

Older Children. For older students (grades 2 through 6), the effect size for oral reading was weak (0.24). This group of students was composed of "disabled" and "low-achieving" readers. The panel states that, "There may have been too few studies of low-achieving readers in the database (only eight) to draw firm conclusions"(2-109). In regard to the outcome for oral reading, the panel questions, "whether the finding is even reliable" (2-133). Considering the small effect size, the few studies involved in the first place and the fact that findings for one entire group of studies are probably not reliable, it is difficult to draw any conclusions about the impact of systematic phonics on the oral reading of older students.

Comprehension

Younger Children. The subcategory of comprehension showed a moderate effect size of 0.51. For younger children, the tests usually involved "extremely short (usually one-sentence) 'passages.' " Often these tests favored "phonetically regular words" (2-107). The comprehension results were based on only one kindergarten comparison and ten first-grade studies, again raising serious questions about reliability. The data suggest that systematic phonics instruction has a moderately significant impact on the comprehension of at-risk kindergartners and first graders, provided the passages are short and that they generally favor phonetically regular words. As with the findings for spelling, we must look to the results for older readers to determine if phonics significantly benefits children when they approach assessment tasks that more closely approximate authentic reading activities.

Older Children. For the older students included in the studies analyzed by the panel, "comprehension of text was not significantly improved" by systematic phonics instruction. (*The Summary Booklet*, p. 9). "However, phonics instruction failed to exert a significant impact on the reading performance of low-achieving readers in 2nd through 6th grade" (2-133). The NRP report continues, "phonics instruction appears to contribute only weakly, if at all, in helping poor readers apply these [decoding skills] to read text and to spell words" (2-116).

The panel's claim that systematic phonics instruction benefits children in kindergarten through sixth grade is incorrect based on its own data! Recall, these are the *panel's* words. These are the *panel's* conclusions—*not mine!*

DID THE PANEL LIE? THE RESEARCH MANIPULATIONS

This is very confusing and the opposite of what we've all heard and seen in the headlines. Didn't the NRP report show that phonics significantly improved children's reading in grades K–6? Did the panel just deliberately misrepresent the results?

Two factors contributed to the extensive misrepresentations of the actual findings. First, you will recall that the results indicate there is a distinct difference in the way children applied phonics to de-contextualized tasks such as reading phonetically regular nonwords such as *dat* or *dit* and their ability (or we could say their *in*ability) to apply those skills to authentic activities. We also saw that spelling for children in kindergarten and first grade accepted invented spellings.

Recall that the NRP conducted a meta-analysis, a procedure that supposedly allows researchers to look across a variety of studies and come to a general consensus about the results, provided that the outcomes are conceptually consistent. Now here is where the panel manipulated the results before it ever even conducted its analysis. The "comprehensive . . . landmark" review of the research on phonics actually consisted of only thirty-eight studies (2-91). Furthermore, the panel decided that the only research it would include would be experimental research as that, so the thinking goes, is the only research that is truly "scientific." Let's think about that for a minute. By establishing that criteria, the research base was narrowed to that which could be dissected, taught, practiced, and tested in isolated, easily assessable fragments. All neat and easy. Not like the messy process of reading as we know it, right?

As mentioned before, some of the studies looked at only one isolated outcome such as decoding or word identification of phonetically regular text. Most of the studies looked at two or three skills taught and tested in isolation instead of more authentic measures of phonics skills such as comprehension and/or spelling (2-92). As we saw earlier, what the panel then did was to name *any* outcome *at all* that a study analyzed "general reading" or "reading growth." Therefore, reading growth could mean only the decoding of phonetically regular words in one study, or, in another, reading growth could be defined as invented spelling or oral reading or even in a few cases as comprehension. Panel member Joanne Yatvin states that the panel used "all kinds of isolated skills, including the decoding of 'pseudowords' and called them 'reading.' "[35]

To reiterate, the majority of the final outcomes for those individual thirty-eight studies that the panel examined were *based on isolated skills*. Some actually looked at only one category, such as word identification or reading nonwords, and yet those outcomes were called General Reading Growth (2-92).

Picture a scale with eighty-four red chips to represent the percentage of study comparisons that looked *only* at isolated skills. Remember, the panel called these isolated outcomes reading. Now add sixteen blue chips, the percentages of study comparisons representing comprehension, to that pile. Each chip contributes equally to the average. We can see that by far the greatest influence on the total are the eighty-four discrete, various and sundry isolated skills. This is what the National Reading Panel called Reading. As we have seen through the analysis, phonics did impact the big pile of chips, the isolated skills that far outweighed our little pile of sixteen chips representing comprehension. We all know that it is entirely possible for children to exhibit mastery of such skills especially when they are phonetically regular, and yet have no comprehension whatsoever. The exact quote, chapter, and page number from the NRP is as follows: "Whereas 76% of the effect sizes involved reading or spelling single words, only 24% involved text reading" (2-111). Of that 24 percent (which included outcomes of oral reading and comprehension) only *16 percent* actually assessed comprehension as an outcome in spite of the fact that the panel determined that application to real reading and writing activities was the essential outcome of phonics instruction.

One reason that the headlines claimed that phonics significantly benefited children's reading is that the majority of the studies in the NRP's meta-analysis relied on isolated subskills instead of on reading as a complex process of which comprehension is an integral part. In the language of statistical research, we say that the *Report of the National Reading Panel* lacked *validity*. That is, the NRP did not base its findings on what it declared to be the essential outcome of phonics instruction—application to authentic reading and writing activities. A second reason for the confusion about the results is that the conclusions drawn by the NRP and their ultimate reporting in the media contradicted the actual findings.

SEPARATE RESULTS FOR KINDERGARTEN AND PRESCHOOL CHILDREN

Sometimes it is difficult to explain results given in a table to parents. Can you explain this in simple lay terms? There is a lot of pressure for "early intervention" based on the results of the NRP. As I look at Table 1 and the results the panel reported, I see that the panel combined kindergarten with first grade. I need to know the results just for kindergarten and preschool children.

In plain English, what this all boils down to is this: The studies in the phonics section did not assess preschool children. The panel was faced with a problem in terms of their kindergarten studies. What you will see from the data I report here is that there were not enough studies on kindergarten children to draw any conclusions. Furthermore, the vast majority of the kindergarten studies applied only to at-risk children. There was only one comparison that even included "normally progressing" children in kindergarten. By looking at these studies and their results you will see that the sweeping claims and mandates being made for preschool children are false.

Findings for Kindergarten Children

Can the results of the NRP be applied to all kindergarten children? No. The results apply *only* to "at-risk" children for whom English is their first language. There were too few studies to merit including kindergarten as a category separate from first-grade.

How many studies were the results for kindergarten based on? Only four studies examined the effects of phonics on kindergarten children. These four studies included seven comparisons, and six of those seven involved at-risk children.[36]

How many kindergarten studies are the comprehension results based on? The results for comprehension are based on only *one* study. Furthermore, the study only required the children to apply phonics to short, phonetically regular passages, and compared children who were intensively trained for twelve weeks to children who were not trained and were part of whole-class instruction. Nevertheless, the results were only a small 0.36. We cannot base policy on only one study using inauthentic text and demonstrating weak results.[37]

Did systematic phonics help kindergarten children to read orally? No. Absolutely not. There were only two kindergarten studies in the NRP that assessed oral reading. *Both* were *not* significant even though the text comprised phonetically regular words. The results did not differ from 0.[38] Nevertheless, all evidence to the contrary, the NRP still reported that phonics helped the oral reading of younger children! Appendix G and previous discussions will verify these statements.

How many studies looked at spelling for kindergarten? The results for spelling for kindergarten were based on only three studies *and* they accepted invented or developmental spellings. As we have seen the documentation for the outcomes for the entire NRP, here is *no* evidence that systematic phonics instruction transferred to conventional spelling. Not at *any* grade level.[39] The results did show that the at-risk children in the studies made moderate gains in applying phonics to invented spelling. Remember, though, this is based on only three studies. More important, as I stated above, the results did not transfer to conventional spelling. In fact, as we have seen in the results for intense phonics in commercial programs, the results as children move to conventional spelling are actually *negative*.

How many studies looked at decoding for kindergarten children and what were the results? Only one study actually looked at decoding for kindergarten children. The results were only moderate even though the children were intensively trained. Furthermore, the results for decoding were based on the performance of children who were trained in small groups. Again, the findings were then compared to untrained children who received whole-class instruction. This represents an uneven level of comparison. It is important to note yet again that the decoding skills did not transfer to reading comprehension on authentic texts that used real words and longer passages.[40]

PANEL'S EXPLANATION FOR WHY ISOLATED PHONICS DOESN'T APPLY TO AUTHENTIC TEXT

Does the Report of the National Reading Panel offer any explanation for the fact that phonics doesn't appear to transfer for older or even for younger children when they need those skills for application to authentic text, as with comprehension and spelling?

Yes, the NRP explains both the reason why many of the studies focused on isolated skills rather than on comprehension as well as why isolated skills instruction doesn't transfer to authentic text. You can use the following explanations taken directly from their report to defend your classroom instruction against a heavy focus on intensive, systematic phonics instruction. The NRP report states:

> The imbalance [of isolated skills outcomes in the NRP studies] favoring single words is not surprising given that the focus of

phonics instruction is on improving children's ability to read and spell *words* . . . (2-92)

The purpose of this practice is centered on word recognition rather than on comprehending and thinking about the meaning of what is being read. This may be another reason why effect sizes for comprehension were smaller than effect sizes on word reading. (2-123)

The results for conventional spelling were not significant because, "as readers move up in the grades, remembering the spellings of words is less a matter of applying letter-sound correspondences and more a matter of knowing more advanced patterns and morphologically based regularities which is not typically addressed in phonics instruction" (2-116).

The NRP report states that phonics instruction does not benefit children with poor comprehension. In explaining the lack of transfer to authentic text, the report explains, "their [the children's reading difficulties] arose from sources not treated by phonics instruction such as poor comprehension . . . " (p. 2-133)

The previous quotes show that children do not transfer phonics skills taught in isolation because such training puts the focus on minutiae rather than the "big picture"—the meaning of the text. Furthermore, the statement on spelling indicates that phonics, with its focus on regular patterns, does not significantly benefit children when applied to conventional spelling. Here it helps to use Susan Neuman's statements in her address to the White House Early Childhood Summit, emphasizing that children need a print-rich environment for the acquisition of skills, and her conclusions recommending that children must be immersed in print to facilitate phonics, phonemic awareness acquisition, and vocabulary and a sense of story.[41]

NRP SUPPORTS USE OF INVENTED OR DEVELOPMENTAL SPELLING

You've mentioned the results for spelling throughout the NRP report and it appears that there is a distinct difference between the impact of phonics on invented versus conventional spelling. There is considerable pressure against the use of invented spelling. How can I defend its use through the research of the National Reading Panel?

First, let's look at what the NRP included in its meta-analysis. All of the studies for younger children accepted invented spellings as being correct. Therefore, the NRP reported its positive results of the impact of phonics on spelling for younger children based on invented or developmental spellings. It's fair to assume that the National Reading Panel would *not* have reported positive findings for a method it did not deem to be acceptable. In other words, the NRP validated the use of invented spellings by accepting and reporting the findings of studies that accepted invented spellings in its meta-analysis. Panel member Joanne Yatvin states that in the behind-the-scenes discussions as well as in its selection of studies, the NRP members believed that children should be encouraged in the use of invented spelling.

I'm very confused. A fellow teacher brought an issue of People *magazine to school. In it is an article focusing on White House/NICHD researcher Louisa Moats. The article, titled "Why Johnny Can't Spel," blames invented spelling and whole language for the decline in spelling ability. Isn't that statement a direct contradiction of the Report of the National Reading Panel that was actually sponsored by NICHD? What's going on?*

This attack on invented spelling and the belief that phonics helps children spell is becoming a common misconception as the "phonics helps spelling" claim is furthered by purveyors of commercial phonics programs. It is important to make absolutely clear that first, the NRP is not opposed to invented spelling, and second, phonics did *not* help children to spell conventionally at *any* grade level.

The *People* magazine article by NICHD researcher Louisa Moats is representative of the false attacks on invented spelling that are so common. I want to address the article as it is published in this popular forum because, as we all know, parents are much more likely to read an article in a magazine on a newsstand than they are to read a documented article in a professional journal. Moats states in her article, "statistics are scarce" on children's spelling ability.[42] Nevertheless, she makes two incredible leaps. First, she claims that there is a decline in children's ability to spell, although she herself notes she has little evidence to substantiate that claim. Second, she blames the purely speculative decline in spelling ability on invented spelling and on the fact that "two decades ago, the prevailing method was phonics, which requires students to memorize the combinations of letters that form the sounds of words."[43]

As we saw earlier, the NRP not only accepted invented spellings but validated its use by reporting invented spelling outcomes as a benefit of phonics instruction. However, if we look beyond the spelling findings for kindergarten and first grade we see yet another error in the claim made by Louisa Moats. This is a *direct* quote from the NRP report: "The effect size [final results] for spelling [for children in second through sixth grades] was not statistically different from zero . . . [phonics was] not more effective than other forms of instruction in producing growth in spelling" (2-116). We have documented repeatedly that there are no data, at any grade level, indicating that phonics helped children to spell conventionally. The studies for younger children accepted invented spellings and the results for all children in grades 2, 3, 4, 5, and 6 showed no significant effect sizes.

Furthermore, as we have seen in the most phonics-intensive commercial programs such as Open Court, phonics instruction actually produced a NEGATIVE impact on children's spelling. That is, after intensive training in phonics, children drilled using Open Court actually did *worse* on spelling than children who received whole language, whole group instruction. The Open Court results were NEGATIVE –0.19!

We find yet another blatant error in the *People* article. Moats, who is fifty-six years old at this writing, admits to being less than a "stellar speller" herself. Given her age and the time period in which she was taught to spell, Moats cannot blame whole language for her problems with spelling. Moats' statements contradict the *Report of the National Reading Panel*, sponsored by the National

Institute of Child Health and Human Development, for which she is a researcher! National Reading Panel member Joanne Yatvin states that in condemning invented spelling, "Louisa Moats is speaking for herself, not for the National Reading Panel."[44]

WHY THE NRP FINDINGS APPLY ONLY TO PROBLEM READERS

One of the points you reiterate throughout the discussion of the NRP findings is that the results can apply only to limited populations of children. Why can't we apply the findings to all students? Why must we only apply the results to "at-risk" readers?

As we've seen previously, important populations of children were not analyzed as groups. They may have been included randomly in treatment or even control groups, but most of the studies singled out children with specifically defined reading difficulties. Among those groups that were not analyzed in the NRP report are children for whom English is a second language (ESL students), sometimes referred to as Limited English Proficiency students (LEP). The studies also did not include enough information on "good" or "high" readers or "normally developing" children for any grade level other than first grade for the result to be relevant to those groups.

What does that mean for those of us who are trying to make sense of the findings?

To answer this question, we need to look at a research term called *generalizability*. When researchers are exploring a question, they cannot possibly include every single person for whom the results could be applicable. They must choose a sample. That sample must represent a *reasonable subset of the population*. Let's look at a large study that we're familiar with—political polls or general public opinion polls, for example. Such polls segment their questions and responses according to particular populations. People respond differently depending on their age, their economic status, and even the area of the country in which they live. Fifteen-year-old girls living in the suburbs will most likely have a different response to Britney Spears, for example, than sixty-year-old women living in the Bible Belt. Similarly, in educational research studies *must* carefully define the characteristics of the populations on which the research was conducted because the results can *only* be applied to similar populations in terms of age, ability, economic status, and most important, language background.

The experimental studies that made up the research base of the NRP report were confined to narrow student populations defined by particular characteristics. The NRP *itself* states that its results apply to only three groups of problem readers. The report *itself* states, "there were insufficient data to draw any conclusions about the effects of phonics instruction with normally developing readers above first grade" (2-116). Furthermore, as we recall, there were only four kindergarten studies in the entire NRP report and those were conducted almost exclusively on at-risk children. Other groups of children such as ESL or LEP students are not even mentioned in the phonics section of the report, so the results cannot apply to them either.

As we saw earlier, the NRP report is fatally flawed in terms of *validity*. The report did not assess what it said it did in that the panel's term *reading growth* was a misnomer, referring to a hodgepodge of isolated subskills rather than to what the report claimed to assess and the panel declared to be important—application to authentic reading and writing activities. Now we see that the report is also flawed in terms of the vital research concept of *generalizabilty* because the studies were directed toward limited student populations and cannot be applied to all students in typical classrooms.

While we're at it, let's look at yet another important research element, *reliability*. In research terminology, reliability is as essential as validity. To be statistically and practically reliable, the instruments used must be dependable, trustworthy, and appropriate for the populations on which they are used. The NRP report states that eight of the studies for older readers were flawed and, therefore, probably not reliable. The exact quote is as follows: "There may have been too few studies of low-achieving readers in the database [only eight] to draw firm conclusions" (2-117), and "the results may not even be reliable" (2-94).

In addition to the eight studies that are probably not reliable, the panel states, "there were only seven comparisons involving older, normally developing readers and four of these came from one study using the Orton-Gillingham method, a program developed for disabled readers, not for nondisabled upper-elementary-level readers" (2-115). There were so few studies with normal readers above first grade (and remember, *below* first grade as well) that the panel determined, "There were insufficient data to draw any conclusions about the effects of phonics instruction with normally developing readers above first grade" (2-116). The bottom line is that the studies used by the NRP were not reliable based on the type of assessments used *and* the fact that there were so few studies involved in the meta-analysis. I include this information here because you may need it.

NRP CAUTIONS AGAINST USING PHONICS WHEN DIALECTS DIFFER

What about ESL and LEP children? You stated that they were not part of the "generalizable" populations. Don't they have unique needs because of their language backgrounds?

Absolutely! So much so that the NRP report issues severe cautions about teaching phonics to ESL children. While ESL students are not even mentioned in the *Report of the Subgroups on Phonics* or in *The Summary Booklet*, the report's "Phonemic Awareness" chapter contains a lengthy, very important warning about using phonics with ESL students or children who have dialects that differ from those of the teacher. First, we will look at what the NRP states about the dangers of teaching phonics to children with dialects that differ from the teacher's. The *Report of the National Reading Panel* warns:

> One important moderator variable that was not considered in
> the analysis is dialect because none of the studies paid attention
> to this variable. However, regional differences at the phonemic

level of language are likely to be important. For example, vowel phoneme categories are not the same across the United States. Some dialects make more phonemic distinctions among vowels than other dialects. Vowels in the three words *marry, Mary,* and *merry,* are pronounced identically in some areas of the West but differently in some areas of the East. As a result, no generalizations about these vowel phonemes will suit everyone receiving PA [phonemic awareness] instruction. Another dialectical difference involves preserving or deleting the final consonants in words, for example, past-tense markers such as the /t/ in *looked.* . . . (2-32)

In my classroom, children come from many different regions. I myself was born and raised far from the area in which I'm teaching. What does this mean for teaching phonics?

Teaching phonics to children with varying dialects can confuse children. The NRP report states:

The fact that regional phonemic variations exist means that teachers implementing PA training programs need to be aware of their students' dialects and whether they deviate from the phonological systems that are assumed in the programs. Ignoring deviations is likely to undermine the credibility of instruction. (2-32)

WHY NRP FINDINGS CANNOT BE APPLIED TO ESL STUDENTS

In addition to having children with regional dialects that differ from my own, I have children in my classes who have first-language backgrounds other than English. One year, I had thirteen different languages represented, and these varied from Hmong, Vietnamese, and Japanese, to Russian, French, and others. The phonological bases for these languages aren't even remotely similar. Doesn't this also complicate phonics instruction?

Again, yes! The National Reading Panel recognizes first-language differences as an enormous obstacle in phonics instruction. The NRP report states:

Another variation related to students' phonological systems but neglected in the analysis is whether English is the first or second language of students. The problem here is that phonemes in English may not be phonemes in ESL students' first language. To understand this requires distinguishing between phonemes and phonics. Phonemes are the smallest units in speech that signal a difference in meaning to a listener who knows the language. Phones are also the smallest units in speech but are described by acoustic and articulatory properties. To perceive phonemes, speakers use categories *that were constructed in their minds when they learned their particular language.* In contrast, phones are defined by their physical properties. Phonemes are broader categories that may include several phones, called allophones, differing in their articulatory features. (2-32)

The terms phones *and* allophones *are unfamiliar to me. What do they mean in practical terms for the children in my class who come from language backgrounds other than English?*

What this means for instruction is that children with different language backgrounds literally cannot hear, much less repeat, much less *apply* many of the phonics sounds that we are teaching! The NRP report states:

> For example, the initial sounds of *chop* and *shop* are articulated differently, so they are two different phones. To an English speaker, they are also different phonemes, because substituting one for the other signals a different word. However, to a speaker of Spanish, the two different phones are the same phoneme. The change in articulation does not signal a different word in Spanish. The speaker either fails to notice the difference or perceives it as a slightly different way of pronouncing the same word. Another example is that Chinese and Japanese speakers process /l/ and /r/ as the same phoneme in English words. (2-32)

So does the scientific research say that even if children do understand the words, they actually cannot even hear, much less distinguish among, much less apply some of the phonemes and phonics sounds I am trying to teach them?

This is *exactly* what the research says in no uncertain terms. The NRP states that children will most certainly be confused by these sounds when they are taught in isolation. Here is a direct quote:

The distinction between phonemes and phones may seem trivial, but it is not. If teachers have students who are learning English as a second language, they need to realize that their students are almost bound to misperceive some English phonemes because their linguistic minds are programmed to categorize phonemes in their first language, and this system may conflict with the phoneme categorization system in English. (2-32)

Will this confusion of phonemes directly affect children's ability to apply phonics skills?

Absolutely. The NRP states:

> Their [children's] confusions will be most apparent when they select letters to spell unfamiliar words. If they know Spanish, they may select *ch* when they should use *sh*. If they know Japanese or Chinese, they may confuse *l* and *r*. When teachers teach [phonics and phonemic awareness] they need to be sensitive to these sources of difficulty faced by their ESL students. (2-32)

Barbara Foorman, one of the pivotal researchers in phonemic awareness and the sole reviewer of the phonics section of the report, actually needed a translator when she administered her research assessments in Texas. She could not distinguish children's pronunciations in some of the regional dialects. She stated:

> When I came to Texas, I was lost. . . . It took me five years and I was right in there being a good Texan with my Southeast Texas dialect. And Houston was an interesting place to study. There were a lot of people from Detroit and New Jersey and all over the place and native Texans, and I always have a native Texan on my research project because they need to tell me that *r-e-a-l* on my word list is pronounced *rill*. I need that person to help me.[45]

That is all well and good for some researcher in Texas, but I have many different language backgrounds and dialects to deal with in my classroom. I don't have the luxury of an army of translators. What can I do?

While the NRP cautions against teaching phonics to children with differing dialectic and language patterns, it does not tell us *how* to deal with the problems. However, there is a body of research available for helping ESL students.

As we synthesize the NRP's own scientific research findings, we see that it is essential to teach skills in a meaningful, contextualized, print-rich environment. Since some children literally cannot hear certain sounds and since they may confuse them because of their own unique regional dialects, we must give children firm, concrete, and meaningful activities on which to "hang their hats." I highly recommend the work of Yvonne and David Freeman and Stephen Krashen for a sound theoretical base as well as for practical teaching suggestions that address the unique needs of ESL students.

There is no easy answer for dealing with the challenges of the many languages in our classrooms. The following list provides suggestions for specific activities that you can consider using with ESL students as a starting point:

- We can focus on language experience approaches, writing the children's own words and sounding them out as we do so, as children watch and chime in. We can do this by writing individual, small-group, or whole-class "daily news" items on an overhead, or even by writing a class letter on chart paper. Phonics skills, punctuation, and spelling can then be explicitly taught, *after* the children have been provided with a meaningful, motivating context. They need to see how it all fits together so that it makes sense. Children are much more likely to understand a sound if they see its connections to letters and how those letters connect to the whole.
- We can use Big Books to immerse children in interesting, motivational print, and draw attention to specific phonics sounds and spelling patterns *after* providing a meaningful context for those sounds.
- We can involve parents. Why not invite them into the classroom and solicit their help in translating texts into children's native languages? Engaging them in this way and forming book clubs, such as those suggested by Assistant Secretary of Education Susan Neuman, is a wonderful way to help not only ESL students but parents as well.

- We can also use children's own writing to help teach spelling, vocabulary, and phonics. I've found that having children circle words in their own writing that they are unsure of is a motivating technique for personalizing spelling instruction, teaching phonics, and moving children from invented to conventional spelling.

- Another technique that works for me is to produce word webs on which we categorize words and provide translations for those words in other languages. I've also found that accompanying those words with pictures drawn by the children and giving them opportunities to dramatize words such as *whispering* or *jumping* helps to establish a concrete, meaningful connection for them and celebrates their own unique language backgrounds.

- I have also used my own sad lack of bilingualism to my advantage. I very explicitly put myself in the position of learner and ask children to translate words from English to their own languages as I write them on our celebratory word wall. I don't believe in asking children or anyone else to take risks, or to put themselves in situations that may be embarrassing to them unless I am willing to take those risks myself. Even though I have mangled other languages almost beyond recognition, I have still tried. And I always turned to children and parents for help.

- I have also made tapes of books. I invite second language learners to listen to books I've read in class on tape. I ask parents who are able to do so to make tapes of the many books that are now available in other languages including Spanish, Chinese, and Hmong. My English proficient students could also listen to them. In time, children can make these tapes themselves to add to our listening center.

- The syntax, or the placement of parts of speech, sometimes differs in other languages. For example, in Spanish and French, descriptors follow the noun they are modifying as opposed to English, in which adjectives *precede* nouns. I make such differences explicit by taking English phrases from a text we have read, color-coding the parts of speech (nouns are blue, adjectives red), and following the phrase with a similarly color-coded translation. For example, a phrase from *The Napping House* by Audrey Wood looks like this in my pocket chart:

A napping house

Una casa adormecida

- I also color-code inflectional endings such as *ed,* and plurals on word walls as some languages such as Hmong do not use inflectional endings. I have found that emphasizing such differences in color helps. It's worth a try.

These are just a few ideas here that can get you started in applying the concepts revealed by scientific research. Of course, these activities are also appropriate for children whose first language is English. If you keep in mind the overarching need to teach skills concretely in a meaningful, motivating context, I'm sure you can come up with your own ideas. Since the NRP offers no suggestions, I felt I needed to offer a few here. Remember, the *Report of the National Reading Panel* states that teachers must make their own instructional decisions. "One size does not fit all." You know your students better than the publishers of commercial programs, better than the National Reading Panel, and better than I do!

DOES THE NRP SAY PHONICS IS APPROPRIATE FOR ALL CHILDREN?

I've found through years of teaching that phonics doesn't work for some children. They just don't get it, or they can't hear the sounds, and yet they do learn to read and write and spell. Must children be taught phonics in order to learn to read and write?

This is a loaded question given the current political environment and the enormous pressures to teach phonics. If you have children in your care who, as you say, are confused by phonics and learn to read using other methods, then you can refer to the statement by Linnea Ehri, confirming that the NRP did not find one best method to teach reading. You can also refer to panel member S. J. Samuels' statement that children are all different and that there are so many variables involved in their backgrounds and learning styles that different approaches are needed.

If you teach above first grade, you can also refer to the results of the NRP report to establish that phonics doesn't significantly impact the reading of children from grades 2 through 6. If you think about it, that makes sense. Most children have been taught at least some phonics. If they haven't gotten the hang of it by the end of first grade, then it appears they just aren't going to. Instead of persisting on teaching ineffectively, it makes sense to explore other avenues to help children with reading.

I am living proof that it is possible to learn to read without phonics. An entire generation of baby boomers, myself included, learned to read with no phonics instruction at all that I recall. The old Dick and Jane basal readers that were used when I was a child relied almost entirely on a sight-word approach. I did learn phonics, but no one taught me. I acquired the knowledge through immersion in print. I got hooked on books, and phonics acquisition was a side effect and maybe a tool I kept in my back pocket when I came across a word I didn't know or when a spelling pattern was applicable. This fact is absolutely irrefutable. I never formally learned phonics until I was working on my master's degree in reading. My personal experience in phonics acquisition confirms the research of Regie Routman. Routman believes as do I, that skills should be taught in context and that immersion in print facilitates their natural acquisition. Her statement eloquently expresses my own experience as a learner and my own discovery as a teacher:

> It has become crystal clear to me—that children learn phonics best *after* they can already read. I am convinced that the reason our good readers are good at phonics is that in their being able to read they can intuitively make sense of phonics. When phonics is isolated as the main method of teaching, students are prevented from utilizing natural meaningful processes. Reading is then viewed as a word-by-word process which is quite inefficient, nonsensical, and frustrating.[46]

Stephen Krashen also believes that children acquire, rather than "learn," language and skills such as phonics and grammar through immersion in motivating, comprehensible texts and safe environments.[47] I will note here that the panel has also confirmed that skills can be acquired, rather than explicitly taught and learned.

I've never spoken with a teacher who has taught for more than a year or two who doesn't have some story that makes her cringe, some act that she wishes she could go back and undo, some child she knows she could help if she had only known then what she knows now. Sadly, I too have several such stories, but one in particular illustrates how deeply ingrained the pressure to teach phonics was, even back in the 1980s when I was a reading specialist. A third-grade girl named Nicky was referred to me simply because she couldn't "do" phonics. She was a fluent reader with moderate comprehension (on our assessments) but when it came to the phonics section of any test she just couldn't do it. I inflicted nearly two years of intensive phonics drill on a child who just couldn't get it, but more important, who just didn't need it. I wish I could find her and apologize.

I'll bet if you think back to your own experience in learning to read, you'll discover that you too really learned phonics *after* the fact. I will also bet that if you are asked what /ea/ says, you will *first* think of a word you know that has that combination of letters in it and *then* figure out the various and sundry sounds that /ea/ makes. You did *not* think "Hmmm. /ea/ makes a long /e/ sound sometimes." This is not a trivial point. It is a very telling observation on the role of phonics. I believe we learn phonics and spelling patterns "inside out." I know that it is heresy to make such an admission in the present political environment in which phonics is being thrust upon us and *any* softening of its importance is seen as treason. If you do decide that phonics is not appropriate for some children or that its focus should be minimized, just remember, you do have scientific research to back you up.

DEFINITION OF PHONEMIC AWARENESS

You've mentioned phonemic awareness, and it is definitely a buzzword. The funny thing is, I've taught dozens of children to read, and yet I've never even heard of it. What is phonemic awareness?

Phonemic awareness (PA) is the ability to segment and blend words into their distinct sounds. *Phonemes* are the smallest units of speech in language. Phonemic awareness deals only with spoken sounds. As soon as letters are introduced, we are into *phonics*. Phonemes are distinguished from *letters* by encasing the letter-sound in question between slashes. For example, /c/ /a/ /t/ indicates the three distinct sounds that combine to form the word *cat*. The NRP also discusses *phones* and *allophones*. I will give you their definition of these two terms, in case you have need for them:

> Phones are also the smallest units in speech but are described by acoustic and articulatory properties. To perceive phonemes, speakers use categories that were constructed in their minds when they learned a particular language. In contrast phones are defined by their physical properties. Phonemes are broader categories that may include several phones, called allophones, differing in their articulatory features. Even thought the allophones differ, speaker/listeners process them as the same phoneme. (2-32)

How does the NRP suggest that I teach phonemic awareness?

The NRP report states that for reading and spelling, students should be exposed to activities that model manipulating phonemes with letters because doing so, "help(s) children make the connection between PA and its application to reading (and writing)" (2-41). In other words, the panel starts with phonemic awareness as a concept separate from phonics, but then blurs the distinction in its research base as well as in its discussion and recommendations.

Again, perhaps because so few teachers were represented on the panel, the NRP doesn't really offer a lot of help for how to actually *teach* what they recommend. However, if we look at the results of the NRP report, we see that it is important to teach phonemic awareness skill (and phonics) in context. Although I didn't know it at the time, I taught phonemic awareness by writing the children's daily news on an overhead as they helped me segment and combine letters to form words by anticipating what letters should come next as a result of the context. For example, I would write, sounding out as I did so, "Dear Boys and __" and then ask them to help me with the next letter. These "write-alouds," as we termed them, were very similar in concept to the strategies children implement in anticipating words through the shared readings of Big Books. Such activities bring in *all* the reading processes.

Remember, you can also justify using such contextualized activities to connect phonics and phonemic awareness by citing the chair of the NRP, Donald Langenberg. Recall his statement that, "By emphasizing *all* [emphasis mine] of the processes that contribute to growth in reading, teachers will have the best chance of making every child a reader" (2-97). Even silly songs and stories that play with words and sounds give children a love of the sounds of language as well as a sense that letters and sounds are not stagnant and that through manipulating phonemes, we have the power to change words.

How much time should I spend on phonemic awareness?

You don't need to spend a lot of time on it at all. In fact, the NRP states, "In the NRP analysis, studies that spent between 5 and 18 hours teaching PA yielded very large effect size. These findings suggest that PA instruction does not need to be lengthy to exert its strongest effect on spelling and reading" (2-41). Over the period of a school year, the recommended five to eighteen hours of PA instruction breaks down to only a few minutes a day. You probably teach at least this much PA as you conference with students in writer's workshop and model writing and spelling for them.

Do I need a commercial program to teach phonemic awareness? Teachers in my school are being pressured to advocate the purchase of not only phonics programs, but of phonemic awareness programs as well. Can I satisfy the

findings of the scientific research and save money by teaching PA myself?

Save your money. The NRP states, "Classroom teachers are definitely able to teach PA effectively." Furthermore, the NRP concludes, "It is important to recognize that children will acquire some phonemic awareness in the course of learning to read and spell even though they are not taught PA explicitly" (2-43). As a matter of fact, most of the studies that the panel used to establish its theoretical base for PA were correlational (2-1). As the NRP points out, correlational studies indicate that there is a relationship between two variables but they cannot be used to conclude that one variable, such as phonemic awareness, *causes* a particular outcome—such as better *reading.* In other words, it could be that better reading *results* in phonemic awareness instead of vice versa. The NRP reminds us, "correlation does not imply causation" (*The Summary Booklet*, p. 12).

At this juncture, we will also recall Assistant Secretary of Education Susan Neuman's research concluding that phonemic awareness, phonics, and vocabulary are acquired through exposure to print. Thus, the NRP report and Neuman's scientific research provide support for Stephen Krashen's conclusion that PA, phonics, and other skills are sometimes acquired naturally, through reading.[48]

In summary, as you read Big Books to children, sometimes going back into the text to point out words and sounds, as you encourage children to form sounds individually as they are writing, and as you model writing for them, you are teaching phonemic awareness. You are including all the reading processes. And you are teaching scientifically!

ERRORS AND MISREPRESENTATIONS OF THE NRP; PANEL MEMBERS' ADMISSIONS TO INCORRECT CONCLUSIONS

As I understand your analysis of the NRP report, you are making two major points. First, you have established that instead of representing accurate, scientific research, the panel's report broke basic research rules. Second, the report's results do not support teaching phonics in K through sixth grade. I'm confused. The findings you report and document contradict what I have seen in the headlines. What's going on?

I need to remind you here, that every point I reveal about the glaring research flaws in the NRP report are documented using the panel's own words and their own data. They are not my opinion. Furthermore, I am not alone in my assertion that the panel was anything but scientific and objective. Nationally known researcher James Cunningham analyzed the NRP report and concludes, "The panel members' determination of what reading research is scientific is not scientific as they themselves define it."[49]

You have yet another powerful defense against the publicized conclusions of the NRP as they are reported in the media and in *The Summary Booklet* and publicity video. Panel members themselves have admitted that the conclusions, as they are reported, are *wrong*. For example:

- Panel member Timothy Shanahan agrees that the NRP misreported its results. In response to my critique of the NRP in *Language Arts Journal*, he states, "Dr. Garan notes the unfortunate mismatches between the NRP report and its *Summary [Booklet]*. I would agree that it is an imperfect and incomplete representation of the report."[50]
- Panel member Joanne Yatvin agrees that the NRP conclusions contradict the facts. She states, "I could see that the stated conclusions, particularly as they were worded in *The Summary Booklet*, did not accurately represent the research findings."[51]
- In response to my article in the March 2001 issue of *Phi Delta Kappan*, the chair of the Alphabetics subcommittee, Linnea Ehri, and NRP contributor Steven Stahl state, "We admit that some of the writing is not as clear as it should be. The author *rightly notes* that conclusions resulting from the distillation process in *The Summary [Booklet]* sometimes lack the

details, qualifiers, and cautions that appear in the more extensive *Subgroups Report*."[52]

In the section that follows, you have at your disposal the documented contradictions of the NRP report, which should be an enormous help in diffusing pressures to comply with the erroneous conclusions.

HOW THE NATIONAL READING PANEL MISREPRESENTED ITS OWN FINDINGS

To understand how the panel misrepresented its findings, I ask that you visualize three separately bound formats. First is the most widely distributed booklet, the neat little thirty-two-page *Summary Booklet* of the results. Second is a brief, neat little publicity video which, like *The Summary Booklet*, extols the virtues of the NRP report without mentioning any of its limitations. Finally is the lengthy *Report of the Subgroups*, nearly five hundred pages in length, replete with data, tables, appendices, discussions, and statistical methodology and terminology. Hidden in that labyrinth of tables, obscured in the rambling contradictory discussion sections, and buried among the data are the true findings of the NRP—as opposed to what found its way into the neat little *Summary Booklet*. Here in the NRP's own words is the truth versus the contradictions.

The Claim in the Summary

"The meta-analysis revealed that systematic phonics instruction produces significant benefits for students in kindergarten through 6th grade and for children having difficulty learning to read" (*The Summary Booklet*, p. 9).

The Contradiction. "There were insufficient data to draw any conclusions about the effects of phonics instruction with normally developing readers above 1st grade" (2-117). This statement directly contradicts the claim in *The Summary Booklet* and on the video that the results apply to the general student population.

Furthermore, the results for children in grades 2, 3, 4, 5, and 6 were *not* statistically significant for spelling, comprehension, *or* for general reading.

The Claim in the Summary

"Across all grade levels, systematic phonics instruction improved the ability of good readers to spell. The impact was strongest for kindergartners and decreased in later grades. For poor readers, the impact of phonics instruction was small . . ." (*The Summary Booklet,* p. 10).

The Contradiction. "The effect size for spelling [for children in second through sixth grade] was not statistically different from zero. . . . [phonics was] not more effective than other forms of instruction in producing growth in spelling" (2-116). There are no data, at *any* grade level, indicating that phonics helped children to spell conventionally. The studies for younger children accepted invented spellings and the results for all children in grades 2, 3, 4, 5, and 6 showed no significant effect sizes. In addition, there were no results reported anywhere for "good readers," a population mentioned only in *The Summary Booklet.*

The Claim in the Summary

The panel's results indicate that " . . . systematic phonics instruction . . . are indicative of what can be accomplished when explicit, systematic phonics programs are implemented in today's classrooms." (*The Summary Booklet,* p. 9).

The Contradiction. "There were insufficient data to draw any conclusions about the effects of phonics instruction with normally developing readers above 1st grade" (2-117). Furthermore, the results applied to only problem readers and cannot be applied to ESL children. In many classrooms, ESL students actually *are* the typical student!

I was shocked that what has been touted as a "comprehensive review" of the research in reading relied on so few studies.

We've all seen the claims that the NRP reviewed 100,000 studies and yet we see that their analysis was actually very narrow. Why is that?

Here we have yet another misleading statement. The panel may have put 100,000 studies into a database, but they most certainly did not personally read, much less analyze, even those studies that they selected to be used in the meta-analysis. The studies were actually turned over to the graduate students of Steven Stahl, one of the panel's contributors. It was these graduate students who analyzed the studies; the highly regarded members of the National Reading Panel did not even see the majority of them.[53] And let's not forget that *because* the panel members monitoring the alphabetics section didn't read and critique the studies themselves, they were not really in a position to identify possible research flaws, contradictions, and errors. In other words, not only is the meta-analysis verifiably flawed, but also the individual studies may be flawed. Thus the "science" is even more questionable.[54]

Why did so few studies make it into the meta-analysis when the field of reading has literally thousands of studies on the subject? If we accept that the panel established rigorous criteria, don't we need to question those criteria if so few studies in the history of the profession were appropriate? Perhaps we need to question the panel's medical model rather than wondering why so few studies met the criteria. Given that hundreds of research studies are conducted yearly, if that model were indeed an accurate tool for assessing the reading process, wouldn't the majority of the professionals in the field adopt it?

As we have seen, some of the sections didn't even adhere to the criteria the panel established in the first place and included studies that were not experimental. Furthermore, the panel made subjective decisions not only in the selection but in the interpretations as well. Here is a *direct* quote from the report that contradicts its own claim to scientific accuracy:

> Where there were too few studies that satisfied the panel's criteria to *permit* a meta-analysis, the panel made a decision to conduct a more *subjective-qualitative* [emphasis mine] analysis to

provide the best possible information about an instructional topic. (*The Summary Booklet*, p. 5)

In fact, the section on comprehension was based on just such a subjective, nonscientific analysis. Too few studies in that section met the panel's original selection criteria (4-42). Recall that the Comprehension subcommittee arbitrarily concluded that its analysis supported direct instruction.[55] On the other hand, it dismissed the hundreds of studies supporting SSR. There were too few studies for both SSR *and* for explicit instruction to meet their selection criteria. However, the panel accepted the nonscientific findings for direct instruction but *rejected* those for SSR. Why? Because the SSR studies were not scientific! While I might not agree that the findings of the Comprehension subcommittee were totally objective, at least it recognized the complexity of the reading process and did what the Alphabetics committee *should* have done. It admitted that the original medical model was inappropriate and unrealistic and that an honest, relevant meta-analysis could not be conducted given the complexity of the reading process, the few studies that were available, and the diversity in each study's respective outcomes.

It sounds as if the majority of the reading researchers don't use the medical model in their studies. Why did the panel decide it was appropriate?

Here we will recall that the majority of the panel was comprised of cognitive psychologists and professional researchers. The vast majority of them are not classroom teachers and never actually taught children to read; consequently, their worldview is colored and shaped by a very narrow, misguided perspective. We all know that children are complex and that learning cannot be broken into little pieces that all fit neatly together in some controlled experiment. If the process of reading were so simple that we could squeeze it into a single formula, then with all the quick-fix, cure-all methods that have paraded across the educational scene, we would have figured out by now how to ensure that "no child is left behind." Oh, and we'd all be doing it, wouldn't we?

Yet another factor can distort the judgment of scientific re-searchers. Because they are only with students briefly—they come into classrooms, experiment on their "subjects," and then leave—they don't experience the complex interactions that color teach-ing and learning. In fact, such complexities are inconvenient and undesirable in experimental research, which, by its very definition, strips away complexities in order to focus on a single, clean "vari-able" and a single, easily measured "outcome." The big picture cannot be a consideration in what experimental researchers do or they could not measure it. Isn't this obvious from the few studies the panel included in its analysis?

Do any of us really believe that out of the thousands of studies that have been conducted in the entire field of research on phon-ics, only thirty-eight were good enough for the panel? And don't forget, the panel itself determined that at least twelve of those studies were of questionable reliability. Most researchers in the field of reading recognize that the reading process is not as cut and dried as the panel would have us believe.

This panel, then, was not by any means a cross-section of the reading profession. Panel member Joanne Yatvin states that certain members of the NRP made virtually all the decisions. Teacher-practitioners such as Joanne Yatvin, as well as the lone parent on the Alphabetics subcommittee, were in a sense token members. The decisions were made by the scientists.[56]

But even though the scientific medical model the panel claimed to use was inappropriate for complex reading behaviors, from what you've documented, the results still don't support their claims. I guess what I'm asking is, "Did they just deliberately misrepresent the findings?"

I guess what I'm answering is, "I don't know." I will say this, how-ever. When panel members are painted into a corner as they were by my published, tightly documented critique of the NRP, they make only vague, general admissions to errors and contradictions.[57] They will not stand up and admit that their research was not valid, reliable, or generalizable, much less that the results do not support the conclusion that "systematic phonics instruction produces significant benefits for students in kindergarten [through] 6th grade and for children having difficulty learning to read." They admit the report contains flaws and contradictions, but they will not themselves delineate what they were. Quite frankly, the panel's admissions to "mistakes" remind me of the vague confessions made by politicians when they are caught in some impropriety: "I'm not perfect. I've made mistakes . . ." without articulating the specific nature of these mistakes or accepting the responsibility for amending them.

But—this panel claims to be "objective." Are their evasions deliberate?

Again, I must say that I don't know. However, there are some facts that we need to address even though it is awkward, even embarrassing to do so. There are questions that are entirely appropriate for us to ask, as this report was funded with our tax dollars and will impact our education system from preschool through university settings.

We all know that in the judicial system, judges and lawyers recuse, or remove themselves from any procedures in which they have even a small personal, professional, political, or financial interest. The purpose for doing so isn't because such involvement establishes wrongdoing. The reason is that in matters of great importance, it is essential that those in control be above suspicion. They must conduct themselves in such a way that there is not even the *appearance* of impropriety. We have the right to expect that panel members claiming objectively would also recuse themselves from research that would advance their own personal interests.

Surely, then, when the panel was established, Congress and the NICHD ensured that the panel represented a truly balanced, objective group of researchers.

Unfortunately, research is not held to the same standard as proceedings in the judicial system. The scientific researchers on the

National Reading Panel had vested interests in the outcome of the report both professionally and, unfortunately, financially.

WHAT SOME PANEL MEMBERS HAD AT STAKE IN THE NRP RESULTS

The Professional Stakes

The professional careers of many of the panel members have been established on experimental research. If they admitted the results of their "landmark study" did not confirm their deeply ingrained philosophies, they would be negating the *lifetime* of work on which their reputations have been built. I'm not suggesting that such bias is even conscious, but let me ask you this: Isn't it difficult to admit that you are wrong in even minor, personal decisions? How many of us could really step back and say, "This evidence shows that virtually everything I've ever accomplished, everything on which I've built my career and professional reputation is irrelevant and just plain wrong"?

The Financial Stakes

Another factor that clouds the credibility of the panel's findings are the financial interests of some panel contributors and the connections of McGraw-Hill Publishing to the Bush administration. I started to make a flow chart establishing the relationships, but I discovered that they are so intertwined it was impossible to do so. It was like trying to establish a "flow" in a plate of worms. I'll start with the contributors to the National Reading Panel and work my way through the connections from the research—to the profits of McGraw-Hill—to the links with the Department of Education and the Bush administration.

Marilyn Jager Adams. Marilyn Jager Adams is a contributor to the NRP. She is the author of the government-sponsored report, *Beginning to Read.* She is also a coauthor of Open Court, published by McGraw-Hill. This government-supported researcher is cited in the Open Court brochure. Adams also coauthored a phonemic awareness program with the sole reviewer of the phonics section of the NRP report, Barbara Foorman.

Barbara Foorman. Ms. Foorman is the primary researcher for the phonemic awareness research project that touts the success of Open Court (coauthored by Adams).[58] Foorman coauthored *Phonemic Awareness in Young Children* with Adams. Foorman is also the author of a commercial program, Scholastic Spelling, that is advertised as being based on research grants sponsored by NICHD, the agency that directed the NRP report (in Taylor 1998, p. 2). Thus far, we have two NICHD researchers who produce studies that misreport the findings that happen to support their own lucrative commercial programs. Adams and Foorman both use government-sanctioned research that is given the stamp of "science" and use that research to actively advertise their own financial interests. Furthermore, on the title page of *Early Interventions for Children with Reading Problems*, the synthesis of Foorman's studies, she thanks "Open Court Publisher for providing materials and trainers."[59] In other words, it appears that McGraw-Hill, which profited from the research, helped support it while the researchers, who profited from the findings, provided the "science." And misreported the results. Now we will document the connections of McGraw-Hill to the "scientific" research promoted by the Bush administration. Before continuing, though, recall what we discovered about the actual outcomes for Open Court as opposed to the claims made by the publisher.

McGraw-Hill Publishing. Recall the Adams–Foorman–NICHD research–Open Court connection. Now let's examine the links between the publisher of the Open Court and Direct Instruction commercial programs, the NICHD researcher-contributors, and the White House. After the inauguration of George W. Bush, one of the first visitors to the White House was none other than Harold McGraw III, chairman and chief executive of the nation's largest K–12 publisher. Such a visit was not surprising since McGraw was on the board of directors of the Barbara Bush Foundation.

McGraw-Hill Publishing gave $1,000,000 to the Hechinger Institute for Education and the media at Columbia University to sponsor an annual seminar (free) to new education reporters. The purpose of the seminars is to provide reporters with "valuable contacts, reporting methods, story ideas, and in-depth background from leading experts on critical issues." Can anyone doubt that these seminars are designed to indoctrinate the press in methods to promote the financial interests of its sponsor—McGraw-Hill Publishing?[60] Such "educational" initiatives may explain the pro-phonics/ back-to-basics slant that permeates the media and "informs" the public. Now we come back to NRP contributor Marilyn Adams, who, as we have seen, is linked to NRP researcher and sole reviewer of the phonics section Barbara Foorman. George W. Bush selected Marilyn Adams and four other McGraw-Hill authors to guide his Texas reading initiative.[61] Now let's continue the Texas–McGraw–research-science–Bush administration links. Also, Secretary of Education Rod Paige has strong links to McGraw-Hill Publishing.

Rod Paige, Secretary of Education. We recall that G. W. Bush is the former governor of Texas and that Harold McGraw was a member of the board of directors of the Barbara Bush Foundation and that four McGraw-Hill authors were consultants for the Texas initiative. Rod Paige was superintendent for the Houston Independent School District. As such, he solicited input from business leaders for strengthening school support services and programs. He launched a system of charter schools that have broad authority in decisions regarding staffing, textbooks, and materials as well as increased testing. All of these initiatives profit McGraw-Hill Publishing. It is not surprising, then, that Rod Paige was awarded the Harold W. McGraw, Jr., Educator of the Year Award for his "service." Rod Paige is now a strong proponent for the "scientific research" sponsored by NICHD, which is replete with McGraw-Hill "researchers" such as Marilyn Adams and Barbara Foorman.[62]

McGraw-Hill's quarterly report, dated July 26, 2001 (which you can get on-line), states, ". . . McGraw-Hill Education's revenue increased 27.7% to $873.9 million over the first six months of 2000,

despite an economy that showed signs of weakening in 2000."[63]
The report credits its "research-based" educational programs for
the increase. Now, let us recall that McGraw-Hill author Marilyn
Adams is one of the contributors to the *Report of the National Reading Panel*. Recall that McGraw Educator-of-the-Year Award recipient Rod Paige is promoting the NRP report as part of the Bush
Education Plan. Recall the connections to Texas and its role as a
"model" of educational "reform." The following is a direct quote
from the McGraw-Hill Annual Report 2000:

> The growth was more dramatic at SRA/McGraw-Hill, where
> sales increased substantially over 1999. *Open Court Reading Col-
> lections for Young Scholars, Open Court Math, Art Collections,* Sup-
> plemental Reading, and Direct Instruction programs all sold well
> in California, benefiting from the state's special funding via AB
> 2519. SRA/McGraw-Hill's Open Court Reading program also
> succeeded in Texas and in open territories in the midwest.
> Reading played an important part in Macmillan/McGraw-Hill's
> increase over the prior year as well. Reading was very strong in
> Texas, where SRA/McGraw-Hill captured 37% of the K–3
> adoption. . . . Glencoe/McGraw-Hill is now competitive in vir-
> tually every subject area. CTB/McGraw-Hill maintained a
> leadership position in the Educational testing industry in 2000
> with sales increasing double digits.[64]

Thus, we have research subsidized by our tax dollars and conducted by researchers with distinct financial interests in the outcomes. Furthermore, as I documented and as the panel members
admit, the findings of the report were inaccurately reported in *The
Summary Booklet*, in the Bush Education Plan, and throughout
the media. Perhaps it was more than altruism that inspired Harold
McGraw III to declare upon leaving the White House on January
23, 2001, "It's a great day for education."[65]

*While there are many connections between the researchers
for the NRP report, McGraw-Hill Publishing, and the
administration of George W. Bush, isn't it possible that the
researchers are not guilty of deliberate misrepresentation to
promote their own financial and professional interests?*

Of course it's possible. The links I've documented here may not have affected the objectivity of the report any more than research directed and paid for by the tobacco industry influenced the findings on tobacco's health risks and the addictive properties of nicotine. The question we need to ask is, who could, who *would* work to produce and report the most accurate, unbiased results—researchers with clear, vested financial and professional interests in the outcomes or truly independent researchers?

In terms of objectivity and professional and financial interests, don't most academics profit in some way from the results of their research? Don't they benefit in the form of professional promotion and articles and revenue from book sales?

You raise an intriguing ethical question. Certainly, those of us who work at universities profit in a sense from research. Don't teachers also "profit" in the sense that they are paid for teaching children? However, the royalties from professional books are extremely small and the sales potential does not even approach the enormous profits from commercial programs that are big money for big business.

There is a much more important distinction to be made between individuals who write books based on their research and the connections we have seen permeating the players in the McGraw-Hill scenario. The research of the NICHD was subsidized by public money—by our taxes—in the name of "scientific objectivity." Research done independently does not become part of national policy and is not forced upon schools. In my mind, that's a big difference.

ON OBJECTIVITY—MY OWN: INTERPRETATION VERSUS VERIFIABLE DATA

You have consistently mentioned "objectivity." Don't you have your own biases? Aren't you, yourself, lacking the very objectivity that you claim is missing in the research of the National Reading Panel?

Of course I have my own philosophy that I'm certain is reflected in the form of biases. Anyone who claims differently is being less than forthright. And that includes the NICHD and the National Reading Panel and McGraw-Hill Publishing and the administration of George W. Bush.

So, given that you admit to a philosophical preference and state that the direction of your work reflects your own biases, why should anyone accept your interpretation of the findings of the NRP or of what you allege is the panel's lack of objectivity?

The material I present is based on the panel's own data and their own findings as well as those of the agents for the Bush administration who are promoting the "science," and includes their admissions that the conclusions contradict their own data. Therefore, I absolve myself of corrupting my presentation of those findings with my own philosophy. The data speak for themselves. Please, get the report, check the citations, and see for yourself.

How would you respond to possible accusations that you have quoted the panel out of context and, in doing so, have yourself misrepresented the findings.

I would say, "What context?" This report is, by the panel's own admission, a contradictory piece of work. The panel itself could not arrive at a consensus as to the direction of the research, the inclusion of studies, or how the data should be interpreted. The "evidence-based findings," the very claim of "science," were breached in the various methodologies employed as well as in the false reporting of the actual data. Consider the statement of researcher James Cunningham in the prestigious scientific journal, *Reading Research Quarterly*:

> Most of the readers of the *NRP Report* will probably find themselves agreeing with at least one of the findings. However, the test of quality for scientific research is whether knowledgeable and *fair-minded skeptics* [emphasis mine] find it persuasive. All research is persuasive to those who already agree with it. No re-

search is persuasive to the person with a closed mind on the subject. The best science has the power to change the thinking of those who previously disagreed with its conclusions but who are fair-minded enough to admit they were wrong once the case has been made. . . . I predict that the *knowledgeable and fair-minded skeptics* [emphasis mine] who change their minds based on the NRP's findings will be few and far between. Too much professional and historical knowledge about teaching reading is ignored, *too little common sense is brought to bear* [emphasis mine], and too little reading research is considered worthy of consultation.[66]

I expressed my confusion at the philosophical and methodological mishmash that permeates the NRP report to panel member Joanne Yatvin. When I tried to establish a *context*, Yatvin's response to me was very telling. She said,

There you go again, looking for logical consistency where THERE NEVER WAS ANY [emphasis Yatvin's]. The passages you cite were written by three different people with three different philosophical backgrounds. There was no explicit agreement by the panel or even by the subcommittee about a theory of reading. You are trying to make sense out a report that is totally illogical.[67]

Therefore, how can I quote out the *Report of the National Reading Panel* out of context when there *is* no context?

If the tables were turned, and you had control, wouldn't you be the one mandating what we teach and how we teach it?

It is easy to be high-minded and sanctimonious in purely hypothetical situations. In the spirit of being as honest as I can possibly be, my answer is, "I hope not." To impose *any* philosophy and usurp the autonomy of *any* professional is the very antithesis of everything that I believe in. I *hope* that if the tables were turned and "our side" prevailed, *we* would not turn into *them*. I don't believe in federal philosophical mandates, even if they are mine.

Isn't it the irony of a democracy that because it is based on freedom of speech and of thought and of religion we must respect the rights of others to disagree with those very values? If I am ever elected President of the United States or if I become the owner of an obscenely powerful publishing company, you are marginally safe from the imposition of my value system upon your rights as a citizen of my domain.

WILL THIS BOOK DO ANY GOOD?
ARE THEY TOO STRONG TO FIGHT?

Sometimes, it all seems hopeless. Even if we use the information that you've provided here, do you think we can really protect our classrooms? Aren't "they" too powerful to even try to fight?

I know how you feel. Many times I want to just throw up my hands and give up too. But I have some hope tucked away in my back pocket and whenever I feel that way, I pull it out and it keeps me going. I ask myself how "they" managed to gain control. It seems to me that those who have power don't usually have to wrestle very hard to get it. They count on a generalized complacency in those over whom they would gain control. Teachers, myself included, are extremely preoccupied with the day-to-day challenges of the classroom. This is true even at the university level. And we should be.

But, "they" didn't usurp control by sitting back and saying, "Oh, what's the use." As I noted at the beginning of this book, we can no longer just shut our doors, not when we are being choked by unrealistic standards, not when our very salaries and even our jobs are threatened by state and federal mandates. And not when those mandates go *against* the best interests of the children we care about.

In California, many of us at the university level "did our own thing" and pretty much ignored the politics around us. As a result, the policy in this state as well as federal policy is not determined by us. *We let it happen.* And now we've had our wake-up call. They counted on our ignoring the politics swirling around us and we complied.

I realize it requires a lot of time and energy to become politically aware, much less active. I believe that another very human factor comes into play as well. Many of us tend to be nonconfrontational. It isn't easy to take a stand against the prevailing culture, to take the risk of being ridiculed or sounding stupid or, God forbid, not being liked.

Let me give you an example. In July 2001 I attended a literacy symposium at Harvard. The conference was designed to encourage attendees, all of whom were university professors, to change their programs to comply with scientific research. The first presentation was by a representative of the Department of Education, who extolled the science of the National Reading Panel. He warned us that the "stakes were upped" and our failure to change our courses and our research directions accordingly would result in the withholding of grant monies. I, of course, had thoroughly analyzed the NRP report and knew every nonscientific error in its five-hundred-plus pages. I wanted to speak out but I was scared to death because I was in an audience of over two hundred people, including a member of the National Reading Panel.

I could feel the perspiration dripping into my eyes. I was trembling, and even my voice was shaking. Turn this book over and look at my picture on the back cover. I'm a little person with a little voice—even on the best of days. Believe me when I tell you that when I took the microphone and spoke out, my voice was hardly more than a quivering little squeak. But I did it. I said, "You are making the assumption that the NRP report is valid, reliable research and it is not." In all honestly, I believe that was one of the hardest things I ever did in my life. And I almost didn't do it. But I did. And now I am proud that I did and would have been ashamed of myself had I remained silent.

Will my speaking out ultimately change anything? Maybe not—but then again, maybe it will. Not one of the two hundred people in the audience spoke a word to help me. But during the break, some members of the audience came up and thanked me.

Just the fact that I objected made it harder for those controlling the conference to proceed unchallenged with their agenda. Ultimately, even if they *do* prevail, at least I didn't give my tacit approval through silence—to what I know is *wrong*.

I believe there is a more practical reason for us to speak out. In addition to wanting to avoid confrontation by raising our squeaky little voices and risking disapproval or looking stupid, we are ultimately worn down by the persistence of others. Think about it. Isn't part of why we want to give up because they have just plain worn us down? Don't those who have the power possess the same human characteristics? Isn't there a chance that *we* can wear *them* down? Why can't *we* at the very least make it difficult for them to take us over?

I'd ask you to do one more thing. Think about what we ask children in our classes to do when they are pressured to comply with what *they know is wrong.* Do we encourage them to go along with the crowd or do we ask them to stand up for their beliefs? How then can we demand anything less of ourselves?

I know that what is happening to education is wrong. I believe that the Reading Wars are no longer about differing philosophies. I believe we are now being manipulated by shameless financial and political forces. And I truly believe that those forces are not in the best interests of children. I may have wasted my time even writing this book. It might do no good at all. But, you know what? When I am old and gray and I'm sitting on my porch, reflecting back on my life, at least I'll have the satisfaction of saying, "I tried." I hope the same for you.

A POSTSCRIPT ON POLITICS AND PENDULUMS

When I first started writing this book, the dedication read "To children who are at the mercy of the pendulum." In the course of writing, I have come to the conclusion that the familiar pendulum metaphor is not only wrong, it is dangerous. First, the idea assumes that we leap onto some methodological extreme, discover it doesn't work, and then naturally drift back to some middle ground before we swing in the opposite direction. The idea of the pendulum suggests that if we just wait out the latest fad, we can maintain our own philosophies and in time, the force will again be with us. In other words, the pendulum metaphor assumes a natural, almost irresistible cycle.

One of the marvels of writing is that we make discoveries and clarify and refine our beliefs through the process. I came to just such an awakening in the process of assembling this little book. I now believe that there is nothing natural, nor is there anything fadlike, about the forces that are robbing us of our professional rights today. The so-called Reading Wars may at one time have truly represented honest differences in educational philosophies, but that is no longer true. Furthermore, I believe it is no longer a fair fight. I've reluctantly come to the realization that the true motives behind the current state and federal mandates for education are blatantly political and shamelessly financial.

The obscene push for high-stakes testing, the glut of standards that have us in a stranglehold, and the so-called "scientific research" being used to justify imposing such formidable restraints on our professional autonomy are couched in high-sounding language, such as "accountability" and "science-based research." It is all about big money for big, big business, particularly for McGraw-Hill Publishing. I believe that these forces are so powerful and so insidious that we can no longer do as we have done in the past— just shut our doors, maintain a passive aggressive stance, and wait for it all to go away.

The pressures are too strong and they are twisted throughout the entire educational system. We are urged to force developmentally inappropriate skills on preschool children. Teachers in many areas must now follow scripts. Thus, they are robbed, not only of their rights to make instructional decisions, but of their very voices. The tentacles of the state and federal government are well on the way to regulating university teacher education programs to move them away from child-centered, meaning-focused approaches to a basic, piecemeal, skills acquisition approach to reading. What is important in all of this, is that these mandates come from the government itself.

Louise Rosenblatt, who was ninety-five years old at this writing, states that in 1938 when she published her book *Literature as Exploration*, the battle against democracy was fought against an outside threat. Today, however, Rosenblatt states, "Democracy is being threatened from within."[68] The enemy stealing our freedom now is the very government that should be fighting to protect it. For this reason, Rosenblatt concludes, we can no longer consider the current educational shift as being cyclic. If we sit and wait and do nothing, the pendulum, if that's what you are comfortable calling it—or the forces that are robbing us of our rights as teachers—are not going anywhere. Unless we speak out, we lose. And children lose.

This book is largely focused on the *Report of the National Reading Panel* and the scientific research that is being used to bludgeon teachers and schools. But it is *really* about helping you to stand up and fight back—*if* you choose to do so. And I know that many of you do. It gives you a tool for talking back to "them" in their own language, and turning their own false science against them.

The following letter was written by Lucy Haab, who has taught kindergarten for thirty years. It expresses more eloquently than I ever could the frustration approaching despair that many of us feel. When we come to the recognition that Lucy has come to, we are at a turning point. We can sink into the learned helplessness that those outside forces have come to count on. We can quit teaching, which they would also welcome. Or we can fight back. Will we win? Maybe not. But maybe if enough of us resist, we can win. And when all is said and done, we will know that we tried.

Here is Lucy's letter. I believe you will see yourself in her words:

A LETTER FROM A TEACHER

I love teaching and I love children, but I am tired. I am exhausted from trying to fight standards, and programs and curriculum changes that are based on some political agenda imposed on children in the name of scientific research-based standards. As a kindergarten teacher I am personally tired of being asked to teach to standards mandated as a "quick fix" by people who are not teachers and who have no idea what is best for children in the long term. THIS IS UNREALISTIC.

I am tired of the attitude that if children have a difficult time learning something at five, let's fix it (and them) and ask them to learn it at three. THIS IS UNREALISTIC. I am tired of the lack of respect shown for young children and for childhood. THIS IS UNREALISTIC.

I am tired of being asked to teach "rigorous" standards which actually deny a child the time to pursue the arts, social and emotional development, language development, personal interests, physical development, a love for learning, and what I would consider true and appropriate learning—all in the name of skill building. THIS IS UNREALISTIC.

I have learned in my years of teaching that young children learn best as *whole* beings over long periods of time and not by the hundreds of piecemeal standards which ignore their total development. I am tired of being asked to ignore the "Whole Child" so I can force feed children a galaxy of standards and skills. THIS IS UNREALISTIC.

I am tired of spending hours giving diagnostic tests that rob us of precious time for more important projects and activities and which tell me nothing that I do not already know. THIS IS UNREALISTIC. I am tired of being asked to push children constantly upwards instead of being able to help them expand horizontally and enrich their intellects, their horizons, their interests and their abilities to create, to learn and to think. THIS IS UNREALISTIC.

I am tired of being asked to dumb down the curriculum in order to focus on skills and tests. My years as a teacher have proven to me that all children do not learn the same skills in the same way at the same time, nor do they learn them out of the context of rich, engaging learning experiences. And I am tired of politicians who know little or nothing about education taking over my profession and telling me how to teach. THIS IS UNREALISTIC.

I am tired of hearing "how no child should be left behind" without addressing the true issues of equity and the real problems. THIS IS UNREALISTIC. And, I am tired of my professional organizations taking politically correct positions which might give them more "perks" and enhance their clout in the political arena instead of strongly speaking out for children, for teachers, for our professionalism. THIS IS UNREALISTIC.

I am tired of politicians, the state, and now the federal government intruding into my classroom and pushing their own commercial interests in the name of "scientific" research. I am tired of protecting children from being exploited for political and financial purposes. I shouldn't have to. This IS NOT JUST UNREALISTIC. IT IS WRONG.

Lucy Haab

NOTES

1. See Susan Ohanian's *One Size Fits Few: The Folly of Educational Standards* and Alfie Kohn's *The Case Against Standardized Testing: Raising the Scores, Ruining the Schools* for a comprehensive review of the impact of standards and testing on children.

2A. Bush 2001.

2B. Bush, p. 5. The section "Rewarding Success and Sanctioning Failure" reads as follows:

   • **Rewards for Closing the Achievement Gap.** High-performing states that narrow the achievement gap and improve overall student achievement will be rewarded.

   • **Accountability Bonus for States.** Each state will be offered a one-time bonus if it meets accountability requirements, including establishing annual assessments in grades 3–8, within two years of enacting this plan.

   • **"No Child Left Behind" School Rewards.** Successful schools that have made the greatest progress in improving the achievement of disadvantaged students will be recognized and rewarded with "No Child Left Behind" bonuses.

   • **Consequences for Failure.** The Secretary of Education will be authorized to reduce federal funds available to a state for administrative expenses if a state fails to meet their performance objectives and demonstrate results in academic achievement.

3. I attended the McGraw-Hill Open Court presentation at the May 2000 International Reading Association and heard the sales representative make this exact claim to an audience of teachers who watched the attendant slick video presentation. The cover of the Open Court Reading promotional brochure reads: "Teaching Every Child to Read: A Success Story."

4. *Directly* following the article chronicling Secretary of Education Rod Paige's address to the International Reading Association on the importance of implementing scientific research in reading instruction in the June/July 2001 *Reading Today* (p. 21) is an ad for the commercial program "Sound Reading Solutions." Perhaps coincidentally, the ad echoes the message by Rod Paige and advertises itself as "The New Scientific Way to Teach Reading. The Only Fully Integrated Brain-

Compatible Reading System." The ad cites the NICHD and the National Reading Panel report to sell its program.

5. The NRP biographies listed here are taken directly from the panel's website at *http:nationalreadingpanel.org*. The National Reading Panel members are: Dr. Donald Langenberg, Dr. Gloria Correro, Dr. Linnea Ehri, Mrs. Gwenette Ferguson, Ms. Norma Garza, Dr. Michael Kamil, Dr. Cora Bagley Marrett, Dr. S. J. Samuels, Dr. Timothy Shanahan, Dr. Sally Shaywitz, Dr. Thomas Trabasso, Dr. Joanna Williams, Dr. Dale Willows, Dr. Joanne Yatvin.

The biographies of the panel members are as follows:

Dr. Donald Langenberg (Chair), Adelphi, Maryland; Eminent physicist and Chancellor of the thirteen-member University System of Maryland since 1990. Has served as the Chancellor of the University of Illinois at Chicago, Deputy Director (and Acting Director) of the National Science Foundation, Professor of Physics at the University of Pennsylvania, and President of the American Association for the Advancement of Science and the American Physical Society. Highly respected nationally and internationally for his leadership capabilities, his ability to forge consensus on difficult issues, and his dedication to education at all levels.

Dr. Gloria Correro, Starkville, Mississippi; Professor of Curriculum and Instruction and Associate Dean for Instruction, Mississippi State University. Highly respected educator and teacher educator in Mississippi and the southeast and south central regions of the country. Credited with establishing kindergarten and early childhood programs in Mississippi, as well as the Mississippi Reading Assistant. Member, National Council of Teachers of Mathematics, Association for Supervision and Curriculum Development, American Association of Colleges of Teacher Education, Association of Teacher Educators, National Association for the Education of Young Children, Association for Childhood Education International, Phi Delta Kappa, and Phi Kappa Phi.

Dr. Linnea Ehri, New York, New York; Distinguished Professor, Ph.D. Program in Educational Psychology, Graduate School and University Center of the City University of New York. Nationally and internationally recognized scientist for her research on early reading development and instruction. Known among cognitive psychologists for her ability to identify aspects of pedagogy that are popular among teachers and to empirically examine the underlying assumptions of the pedagogy. Past President, Society for the Scientific Study of Reading; past Vice President, American Research Association (Division C-Learning and Instruction); past member, Board of Directors of the National Reading Conference; recipient of the Oscar S. Causey Award for Distinguished Research (National Reading Conference). Member, International Reading Association, Reading Hall of Fame, National Reading Conference, American Educational Research Association, American Psychological Association (Fellow), and Society for the Scientific Study of Reading.

Mrs. Gwenette Ferguson, Houston, Texas; Reading Teacher, North Forest Independent School District (Houston). Chair, English Language Arts Department; Kirby Middle School Teacher of the Year (1991). Received the Kirby Middle School Award for Outstanding Dedication and Service (1988, 1989, 1990); Houston Area Alliance of Black School Educators Outstanding Educator Award, and North Forest Independent School District Achieving Through Excellence Award. Member, National Council of Teachers of English, Texas Council of Teachers of English. Vice President Elect of Affiliates, North Forest District Reading Council, Greater Houston Area Reading Council, and Texas Classroom Teachers Association.

Ms. Norma Garza, Brownsville, Texas; Certified Public Accountant for Law Firm of Rodriguez, Colvin & Chaney, LLP. Founder and chair of the Brownsville Reads Task Force. Serves on the Governor's Focus on Reading Task Force, Governor's Special Education Advisory Committee, Texas panel member of Academics Goals 2000. Received the Texas State Board of Education "Heroes for Children" Award. Member, International Dyslexia Association. Strong advocate for business community involvement in education.

Dr. Michael Kamil, Stanford, California; Professor of Psychological Studies in Education and Learning, Design, and Technology, School of Education, Stanford University. Chair, Stanford University Commission on Technology in Teaching and Learning Grants Committee; Chair, Technology Committee of the National Reading Conference (NRC). Former member of the Board of Directors of the National Reading Conference and the National Conference for Research in English. Former Editor of the Journal of Reading Behavior (1988–89); Editor *NRC Yearbook* (1980–82) and Coeditor, *Reading Research Quarterly* (1991–95). Coauthored *Understanding Research in Reading and Writing* and coedited Volumes I and II of *The Handbook of Reading Research*. Received Albert J. Kingston Award from the National Reading Conference and the Milton Jacobson Readability Research Award from the International Reading Association. Current member of the American Psychological Association, American Educational Research Association, International Reading Association, National

Conference for Research in English (Fellow), and the National Reading Conference.

Dr. Cora Bagley Marrett, Amherst, Massachusetts; Vice Chancellor for Academic Affairs and Provost, University of Massachusetts–Amherst. As Assistant Director, National Science Foundation (1992–1996), was first person to lead the Directorate for Social, Behavioral and Economic Sciences. Also served as Director of the United Negro College Fund/Mellon Programs; Associate Chairperson for Department of Sociology, University of Wisconsin; and member, Board of Directors, Center for Advanced Study in the Behavioral Sciences. Served in 1979 on the President's Commission on the Accident at Three Mile Island. Member, Board of Governors, Argonne National Laboratory; Board of Directors, Social Science Research Council; Commission on the Behavioral and Social Sciences and Education, National Research Council; Peer Review Oversight Group for the National Institutes of Health; National Advisory Council for the Fogarty International Center, also of the National Institutes of Health. Fellow, American Association for the Advancement of Science, and Vice President, American Sociological Association.

Dr. S. J. Samuels, Minneapolis, Minnesota; Professor, Department of Educational Psychology, University of Minnesota. Recipient of the College of Education Distinguished Teaching Award. Internationally respected reading researcher. Highly experienced consultant to inner-city schools. Selected for the Reading Hall of Fame. Received the Wm. S. Gray Citation of Merit from the International Reading Association and the Oscar S. Causey Award from the National Reading Conference for Distinguished Research in Reading. Member of the Governing Council, Center for Research in Perception, Learning and Cognition at the University of Minnesota; American Educational Research Association; American Psychological Association (Fellow); International Reading Association; and National Reading Conference.

Dr. Timothy Shanahan, Chicago, Illinois; Professor of Urban Education, Director of the Center for Literacy, and Coordinator of Graduate Programs in Reading, Writing, and Literacy at the University of Illinois at Chicago. Internationally recognized reading researcher with extensive experience with children in Head Start, children with special needs, and children in inner-city schools. Editor of the yearbook of the National Reading Conference and formerly Associate Editor of the *Journal of Reading Behavior*. Received the Albert J. Harris Award for Outstanding Research on Reading Disability and the Milton D. Jacobson Readability Research Award from the International Reading Association. Member, Board of Directors of the International Reading Association. Member, American Educational Research Association, National Council on Research in Language and Literacy, National Council of Teachers of English, National Reading Conference, and Society for the Study of Reading.

Dr. Sally Shaywitz, New Haven, Connecticut; Professor of Pediatrics and Codirector, Yale Center for the Study of Learning and Attention, Yale University School of Medicine. Neuroscientist nationally and internationally recognized for research contributions in reading development and reading disorders, including recent demonstration of neurobiological substrate of reading and reading disability. Unique for contribution to development of conceptual model of reading and reading disability and for identifying high prevalence of reading disability in girls. Received Distinguished Alumnus Award, Albert Einstein College of Medicine. Most recently served on National Academy of Sciences Panel on Preventing Reading Difficulties in Children. Diplomate, American Board of Pediatrics; member, Institute of Medicine of the National Academy of Sciences, American Academy of Pediatrics, American Association for the Advancement of Science, American Educational Research Association, Council for Exceptional Children, International Dyslexia Association, Society for Developmental and Behavioral Pediatrics, Society for Pediatric Research, Society for Research in Child Development, and Society for the Scientific Study of Reading.

Dr. Thomas Trabasso, Chicago, Illinois; Irving B. Harris Professor, Department of Psychology, The University of Chicago. Cognitive scientist internationally recognized for investigations of comprehension during reading. Has most recently developed a connectionist model that simulates dynamic processing over the course of reading. Has served as Chair of Department of Psychology, Editor of *Cognitive Psychology*, and Associate Editor of the *Journal of Experimental Child Psychology*. Member, Psychonomic Society, Society for Research in Child Development, American Educational Research Association, International Reading Association, National Conference, American Psychological Society, Society for Discourse and Text Processing (Founding Member and Chair), and Society for the Scientific Study of Reading.

Dr. Joanna Williams, New York, New York; Professor of Psychology and Education, Columbia University. Internationally recognized scholar for research on linguistic, cognitive, and perceptual bases of reading development and disorders. Fulbright Scholar, University of

Paris; Oscar S. Causey Award for Outstanding Contributions to Reading Research from the National Reading Council; elected to Reading Hall of Fame (1994); and recognized as a Guy Bond Scholar by the University of Minnesota (1997). Currently serves as Editor of Scientific Studies in Reading and has served as the Editor of the *Journal of Educational Psychology*. Member, American Educational Research Association, American Psychological Association (Fellow), Council for Exceptional Children, International Reading Association, National Conference on Research in English, National Reading Conference, New York Academy of Sciences, and Society for the Scientific Study of Reading.

Dr. Dale Willows, Toronto, Ontario, Canada; Professor, Department of Human Development and Applied Psychology, Ontario Institute for Studies in Education, University of Toronto. Internationally recognized scholar in reading development and reading difficulties. Has served on the editorial boards of the Journal of Research on Reading and Reading Research Quarterly. Member, Educational Research Association, International Dyslexia Association, International Reading Association, and National Reading Conference.

Dr. Joanne Yatvin, Portland, Oregon; Principal, Cottrell and Bull Run Schools, Boring, Oregon. Forty-one years of experience as a classroom teacher and school administrator. Served as Chair of the Committee on Centers of Excellence for English and the Language Arts, National Council of Teachers of English. President of the Wisconsin Council of Teachers of English and the Madison (Wisconsin) Area Reading Council, and a member of the National Advisory Board, Educational Information Center on Reading and Communication Skills ERIC/RCS. Named Elementary Principal of the Year by the Wisconsin Department of Public Instruction and the Wisconsin State Reading Association. Received the Distinguished Elementary Education Alumni Award from the University of Wisconsin School of Education. Member, National Council of Teachers of English, International Reading Association, Association for Supervision and Curriculum Development, and Oregon Reading Association.

6. *The Summary Booklet*, p. 1. The determination to impose the results on classrooms is reiterated in the April 13, 2000 press release by Duane Alexander, Director of NICHD and Donald Langenberg, chair of the NRP. Note: This thirty-two-page summary, separately bound and distributed, has no distinguishing title. I have designated it as *The Summary Booklet* in order to distinguish it from the Subgroups Report.

7. *The Summary Booklet,* p. 5.

8. Cunningham 2001. Cunningham provides a historical research perspective on the definition of "science" and its evolving role in research. He concludes that on its own terms, the NRP fails.

9. The panel used a variety of isolated skills as various and sundry dependent variables. In fact, only 24% of the studies even included reading of text: "Although each comparison could contribute up to six effect sizes, one per outcome measure, few studies did. The majority (76%) of the effect sizes involved reading or spelling single words while 24% involved text reading" (pp. 2–84 or 2–92, depending on which version of the report you are working from). This statement is repeated at least three times throughout the report.

Furthermore, of that 24 percent, only 16 percent of the effect sizes used as dependent variables actually used comprehension as an outcome. The actual breakdown taken from Table G is as follows:

word id = 59 comparisons

decoding = 30 comparisons

spelling = 37 comparisons

comprehension =35 comparisons

nonword = 39 comparisons

oral reading =17 comparisons

If we combine oral reading and comprehension we get 52 comparisons. The grand total is 217. Thus text reading (combining oral reading and comprehension) comes to 24 percent of the total comparisons. However, only 35/217 actually involved "comprehension." This means that only 16 percent of the total studies looked at comprehension. The term *total reading* or *reading growth* as it is used by this panel is a gross misnomer. It can and did refer to studies that used a single, isolated subskill as an outcome. None of the studies included all of the subcategories from isolated skills through comprehension.

My article "Beyond the Smoke and Mirrors: A Critique of the National Reading Panel Report on Phonics" in the March 2001 issue of *Phi Delta Kappan* documents the errors and inconsistencies in the report. See also, the September 2001 issue of *Language Arts Journal* for further information on the flaws and findings of the NRP report.

10. *The Summary Booklet,* p. 8.

11. Both quotes by Linnea Ehri are from The International Reading Organization's bimonthly newsletter, *Reading Today,* June/July 2000. The interview appeared on the front page in the article "National Reading

Panel Report: Work Praised, but Distortion Fears Persist." It appeared shortly after the release of the NRP report and was an attempt to quash the flood of criticism directed at the report. Ehri's statement on whole language in its entirety reads, "Ehri also said that although the report states that systematic instruction in phonemic awareness and phonics helps beginning and struggling readers to read more effectively, 'this does not mean that teachers should abandon whole language practices but rather that they should enrich this approach with systematic phonics instruction.' " I did not include the part on the benefit of systematic phonics instruction because as I document, the report did not support the premise that children transfer isolated, systematic phonics instruction to authentic reading and writing activities.

12. Samuels 1984, p. 390.

13. *Report of the Subgroups*, Appendix G. See studies No. 52 and 59. In order to verify this and other results provided here, I have included Appendix G at the end of this book (see Appendix A).

14. Neuman, July 27, 2001. Her speech at the White House Summit for Early Childhood Cognitive Development was based on an article she coauthored with Donna Celano the Jan/Feb/Mar 2001 issue of *Reading Research Quarterly*. Her speech is well worth reading in its entirety.

15. Neuman 2001.

16. Neuman 2001.

17. Stanovich 1986.

18. Stephen Krashen has helped the panel by analyzing studies that it overlooked. His scientific, statistical analysis confirms the findings of Neuman and Celano: Reading begets more reading and more reading begets skills including phonemic awareness, phonics, and vocabulary (Krashen 2001).

19. Neuman 2001.

20. Cunningham 2001, p. 333.

21. Cunningham 2001, p. 333.

22. Neuman 2001.

23. Neuman and Celano 2001, p. 24.

24. Neuman and Roskos 1997.

25. Neuman 2001.

26. This quote is in the "Minority View" of the NRP. It is located at the end of the report and begins with the numeral 1 as opposed the other page numbers in the report, which are prefaced with the chapter number followed by the page number.

27. Neuman 2001.

28. Timothy Shanahan made this statement on the NRP publicity video that is also available free from the NRP website.

29. For an in-depth discussion of how standardized curricula harms children see Ohanian 1999. See also Kohn 2000.

30. Neuman 2001.

31. The single study that examined Open Court is Study No. 11 (Foorman et al. 1999).

32. See Study No. 11 in Appendix G (see Appendix A) for confirmation of the breakdown of effect sizes for subcategories across grade levels.

33. Study No. 72 (Gersten, Darch, and Gleason 1988).

34. Oakland et al. 1998.

35. Yatvin, J. 2001, p. 801.

36. The four studies that were conducted on kindergarten children were: Study No. 4 (Bond et al. 1995–1996); Study No. 38 (Martinussen and Kirby 1998); Study No. 54 (Vandervelden and Siegel 1997); and Study No. 74 (Stuart 1999). Two other studies began in kindergarten but continued over a period that extended beyond kindergarten. Therefore, the results could not be applied to kindergarten children. These were Study No. 3 (Blachman et al. 1999) that was posttested on children in second or third grade; and Study No. 51 (Torgeson et al. 1999) that started in kindergarten but was posttested on children in the middle of second grade.

37. The one study that examined the effects of phonics on the comprehension of kindergarten children was study No. 74 (Stuart 1999). It involved twelve weeks of extensive tutoring. The results were compared to whole class instruction.

38. The studies that looked at oral reading for kindergarten children were studies No. 4 (Bond et al. 1995) and No. 54 (Vandervelden and Siegel 1997). The results were 0.09 and 0.15 respectively.

39. The two studies that looked at spelling for kindergarten were studies No. 38 (Martinussen and Kirby 1998), Study No. 54 (Vandervelden and Siegel 1997), and Study No. 74 (Stuart 1999).

40. The single study that looked at decoding for kindergarten children was Study No. 38 (Martinussen and Kirby 1998).

41. Neuman 2001.

42. Moats 2001, p. 111.

43. Moats 2001, p.112.

44. Joanne Yatvin made this statement in an interview on August 19, 2001.

45. Taylor 1998, p. 74. This quote by Foorman is from a transcript of the presummit meeting of Governor Bush's Business Council at the Governor's first Reading Summit that took place in Austin, Texas, on April 26, 1996.

46. Routman 1988, p. 44.

47. Krashen 1992.

48. Krashen 1999.

49. Cunningham 2001, p. 328.

50. Shanahan 2001, p. 68.

51. Yatvin 2001, p. 801.

52. Ehri and Stahl 2001, pp. 17–20.

53. From an email interview, August 15, 2001. Yatvin substantiates this statement with her notes, minutes from NRP meetings.

54. For a detailed critique of the Foorman Study, see Gerald Coles' *Misreading Reading: The Bad Science That Hurts Children* (2000). Coles has critiqued the individual studies in the NRP. For his analysis, see *Misguided Research*.

55. Cunningham 2001, p. 334.

56. From an interview with J. Yatvin, August 15, 2001.

57. Linnea Ehri and Steven Stahl admit to errors in "Beyond the Smoke and Mirrors: Putting Out the Fire." My documentation of the errors in their rebuttal is in the same issue of *Phi Delta Kappan* (September 2001). In the September 2001 *Language Arts Journal*, panel member Timothy Shanahan also admits to errors and contradictions.

58. Foorman et al.'s. 1998 phonemic awareness study (study No. 11) is one of the studies included in the NRP. In spite of the negative outcomes for application to authentic text (for the subcategories of spelling and comprehension for second graders) Foorman stated that the children in the Open Court/Direct Instruction group outperformed the district's existing curriculum. See Taylor 2001, p. xviii.

59. Business Wire, Washington, January 23, 2001.

60. Hechinger News. Spring 2001. Published by the Hechinger Institute on Education on the Media, Teachers College, Columbia University. Winter/Spring 1999/2000.

61. Taylor 1998, pp. 4, 64, and 84–85. In addition to Marilyn Adams, other McGraw-Hill authors who were consulted were Douglas Carnine, who has long been associated with DISTAR (Direct Instruction), Jean Osborne, who is associated with Reading Mastery, which is the latest version of DISTAR, and Bonnie Grossman, who is associated with Direct Instruction.

62. This information is available on the Department of Education website as well as the Rod Paige website.

63. McGraw-Hill Annual Report 2000, p. 28.

64. McGraw-Hill Annual Report 2000, p. 29. This information can be obtained by writing to the company or from the McGraw-Hill website.

65. Business Wire, Washington. Press Release, January 23, 2001.

66. Cunningham 2001, p. 335.

67. From an email interview with J. Yatvin. August 22, 2001.

68. Rosenblatt 2001. Rosenblatt made this statement at the AERA Convention in Seattle WA. The title of the presentation was "Democracy and Education: Losing the Battle."

APPENDIX A:
STUDIES IN THE PHONICS DATABASE, THEIR CHARACTERISTICS, AND EFFECT SIZES
(Appendix G of the NRP)

	Characteristics of Training				Characteristics of Part.				Features of Design			Effect Sizes on Post-tests							
Author and Year, Treatment	Type of Phonics	Control Group	Tr.unit	Length of Training	Grade/ Age	Reading Ability	SES	Group Assign.	Sig Pre- test Diff	Total N	Time of Post-test	Mean	Word ID	Dec	Spell	Comp	Nonw	Oral Read	Gen. Read
03 - Blachman et al., (1999)	·	·	·			·		·	·	·	·	·	·	·	·	·	·	·	·
Blachman PA	Syn	Basal	SmG	2-3yrs(41s-.20m/d)	K	AR	Low	NE	No	159	Imm.	0.72	-0.17	1.08	0.94		1.04		
Blachman PA				(1st gr=30 m/d)						128	2nd yr tr.	0.64	0.35	0.81	0.53		0.86		
Blachman PA				(2nd gr=30 m/d)						106	3rd yr tr.	0.36	0.42	0.55	0		0.45		
04 - Bond et al., 1995																			
Sing, Spell, Read, Write	Syn	Basal	Class	1 yr(20 lessons)	K	N	Var	NE	No	144	Imm.	0.51	0.38				1.01	0.13	
Sing, Spell, Read, Write	Syn	Basal	Class	1 yr.	1st	N	Var	NE	No	276	Imm.	0.25	0.23		0.14		0.6	0.03	
Sing, Spell, Read, Write	Syn	Basal	Class	1 yr.	2nd	N	Var	NE	No	320	Imm.	0.38	0.44		0.18		0.55	0.33	
05 - Brown & Felton, 1990																			
Lippincott	Syn	Wh.W.	SmG	2 yrs.	1st	AR	NG	R	No	47	Imm.	0.48	0.02		0.51		0.92		
Lippincott											2nd yr tr.	0.52	0.51	0.63	0.38		0.55		
08 - Eldredge, 1991																			
Modified Whole Language	Syn	Basal	Class	1 yr. (15m/d)	1st	AR	Low	NE	No	105	Imm.	0.63				0.83	0.43		
09 - Evans, 1985																			
Traditional Basal	Misc	Wh.L.	Class	1 yr.	1st	N	Var	NE	NG	20*(N=-247)	Imm.	0.6				0.6			

Appendix G
Studies in the Phonics Database, Their Characteristics, and Effect Sizes
(*Note:* key to this chart is on page 2-176)

Author and Year, Treatment	Characteristics of Training				Characteristics of Part.			Features of Design				Effect Sizes on Post-tests							
	Type of Phonics	Control Group	Tr.unit	Length of Training	Grade/Age	Reading Ability	SES	Group Assign.	Sig Pre-test Diff	Total N	Time of Post-test	Mean	Word ID	Dec	Spell	Comp	Nonw	Oral Read	Gen. Read
11 - Foorman et al., 1998																			
Open Court	Syn	Wh.L.	Class	1 yr. (30m/d)	1st	AR	Var	NE	NG	68	Imm.	0.91	1.63	1.14	0.56	0.32			
Embedded	LU	Wh.L.	Class	1 yr.	1st	AR	Var	NE	NG	70	Imm.	0.36	0.56	0.51	0.26	0.1			
Open Court	Syn	Wh.L.	Class	1 yr.	2nd	LA	Var	NE	NG	35	Imm.	0.12	0.52	0.32	-0.19	-0.19			
Embedded	LU	Wh.L.	Class	1 yr.	2nd	LA	Var	NE	NG	57	Imm.	0.03	0.37	0.22	-0.25	-0.24			
12 - Foorman et al., 1991																			
Synthetic basal	Syn	Wh.W.	Class	1 yr. (45 m/d)	1st	N	Mid	NE	No	6'(N=8-0)	Imm.	2.27	1.92	2.67	2.21				
13 - Foorman et al., 1997																			
Orton-Gillingham	Syn	Wh.W.	SmG	1 yr. (60 m/d)	gr 2-3	RD	Mid	NG	Yes	67	Imm.	0.27	0.17	0.58	0.05				
Onset-rime	LU	Wh.W.	SmG	1 yr.	gr 2-3	RD	Mid	NG	Yes	85	Imm.	-0.11	-0.19	0.09	-0.23				
15 - Fulwiler & Groff, 1980																			
Lippincott	Syn	Wh.W.	Class	1 yr.	1st	N	NG	NE	NG	147	Imm.	0.84		0.91		0.76			
17 - Gittelman & Feingold, 1983																			
Intersensory Method	Syn	Misc.	Tutor	18 wks.(54s)	7-13yr	RD	Mid	R	No	56	Imm.	0.53	0.76	0.67	0.12	0.57			
18 - Greaney et al., 1997																			
RRD-Rime analogy	LU	Wh.W.	Tutor	11 wks.(31s,3-0m)	gr 2-5	LA	NG	R	No	36	Imm.	0.37	0.39				0.51	0.2	
RRD-Rime analogy										34	follow up	0.56	0.47				0.76	0.44	

Appendix G (continued)

Author and Year, Treatment	Type of Phonics	Control Group	Tr.unit	Length of Training	Grade/ Age	Reading Ability	SES	Group Assign.	Sig Pre-test Diff	Total N	Time of Post-test	Mean	Word ID	Dec	Spell	Comp	Nonw	Oral Read	Gen. Read
22 - Haskell et al., 1992																			
Analyze Onset-Rimes	Misc	Wh.W.	SmG	6 wks(15s, 20m)	1st	N	Mid	R	No	24	Imm.	0.14	0.2	0.09					
Analyze Phonemes	Misc	Wh.W.	SmG	6 wks(15s, 20m)	1st	N	Mid	R	No	24	Imm.	-0.07	-0.08	-0.06					
26 - Klesius et al., 1991																			
Traditional Basal	Misc	Wh.L.	Class	1 yr.	1st	N	Var	NE	Yes	6'(N=1-12)	Imm.	0.2			0.36	0.18	0.07		
28 - Leach & Siddall, 1990																			
Direct Instruction	Syn	Misc.	Tutor	10 wks (15m/d)	1st	N	NG	R	No	20	Imm.	1.99				1.8		2.18	
29 - Leinhardt & Engel, 1981																			
NRS-study 2 (Beck)	Syn	Basal	SmG	1 yr.	1st	N	NG	NE	Yes	187	Imm.	0.45	0.45						
NRS-study 3 (Beck)	Syn	Basal	SmG	1 yr.	1st	N	NG	NE	Yes	263	Imm.	0.44	0.44						
NRS-study 4 (Beck)	Syn	Basal	SmG	1 yr.	1st	N	NG	NE	Yes	256	Imm.	0.33	0.33						
NRS-study 6 (Beck)	Syn	Basal	SmG	1 yr.	1st	N	NG	NE	Yes	241	Imm.	0.7	0.7						
32 - Lovett et al., 1989																			
Decoding Skills	Syn	Misc.	SmG	40 ses (33-40h)	8-13yr	RD	Mid	R	No	118	Imm.	0.39	0.78	0.7	0.42	0.07	0.1	0.27	
33 - Lovett & Steinbach, 1997																			
Lovett Analogy	LU	Misc.	SmG	9wks (35h)	gr 2/3	RD	NG	R	No	28	Imm.	0.49	-0.12	0.85			0.75		
Lovett Analogy	LU	Misc.	SmG	9wks (35h)	gr 4	RD	NG	R	No	22	Imm.	1.41	0.84	2.06			1.33		

Appendix G (continued)

Author and Year, Treatment	Characteristics of Training				Characteristics of Part.					Features of Design		Effect Sizes on Post-tests							
	Type of Phonics	Control Group	Tr.unit	Length of Training	Grade/Age	Reading Ability	SES	Group Assign.	Sig Pre-test Diff	Total N	Time of Post-test	Mean	Word ID	Dec	Spell	Comp	Nonw	Oral Read	Gen. Read
Lovett Analogy	LU	Misc.	SmG	9wks (35h)	gr 5/6	RD	NG	R	No	24	Imm.	-0.25	-0.49	-0.15			-0.1		
Lovett Direct Instruction	Syn	Misc.	SmG	9wks (35h)	gr 2/3	RD	NG	R	No	32	Imm.	0.24	0.02	0.24			0.46		
Lovett Direct Instruction	Syn	Misc.	SmG	9wks (35h)	gr 4	RD	NG	R	No	25	Imm.	1.42	1.03	1.53			1.7		
Lovett Direct Instruction	Syn	Misc.	SmG	9wks (35h)	gr 5/6	RD	NG	R	No	27	Imm.	0.09	-0.24	0.25			0.25		
34 - Lovett et al., 1990																			
Analytic	Misc	Misc.	SmG	9wks (35h)	7-13yr	RD	Mid	R	NG	36	Imm.	0.16	0.13	0.11	0.23				
35 - Lum & Morton, 1984																			
Spelling Mastery	Misc	Rg.cls.	Class	1 yr.(20-30 m/d)	2nd	N	NG	NE	No	36	Imm.	0.38	0.31		0.45				
36 - Mantzicopoulos et al., 1992																			
Phonetic read/spell	Misc	Rg.cls.	Tutor	50s (1h/wk)	1st	AR	Mid	R	No	112	Imm.	0.53					0.53		
Phonetic read/spell										112	follow up	0.32		0.33	0.3	0.08	0.56		
37 - Marston et al., 1995																			
Direct Instruction	Syn	Rg.cls.	Class	10 wks (45m/d)	gr 1-6	LA	NG	NE	Y/Adj	53	Imm.	0.01						0.01	
38 - Martinussen & Kirby, 1998																			
Successive phonics	Syn	Rg.cls.	SmG	8 wks(40-60m/wk)	K	AR	NG	R	No	26	Imm.	0.62	0.53	0.63	0.68		0.62		
41 - Oakland et al., 1998																			
Orton-Gillingham	Syn	Rg.cls.	SmG	2 yrs.(350h)	M=11y	RD	NG	NE	Yes	48	2nd yr. tr.	0.54	0.71	0.23	0.23	0.62	0.61		

Appendix G (continued)

| | Characteristics of Training | | | | Characteristics of Part. | | | | Features of Design | | | Effect Sizes on Post-tests | | | | | | | |
Author and Year, Treatment	Type of Phonics	Control Group	Tr.unit	Length of Training	Grade/ Age	Reading Ability	SES	Group Assign.	Sig Pre-test Diff	Total N	Time of Post-test	Mean	Word ID	Dec	Spell	Comp	Nonw	Oral Read	Gen. Read
44 - Santa & Hoien, 1999																			
RRD-Early Steps	LU	Wh.L.	Tutor	1 yr.(30m/d)	1st	AR	Var	NE	No	49	Imm.	0.76	0.93	.	0.63	0.73			.
RRD-Early Steps										41	follow up	0.86	0.57		.	0.87	1.15		
47 - Silberberg et al., 1973																			
Lippincott	Syn	Wh.W.	SmG	1 yr.	gr 3	RD	NG	NE	Yes	69	Imm.	0.5	0.7	.		0.36	.	0.45	.
Orton-Gillingham	Syn	Wh.W.	SmG	1 yr.	gr 3	RD	NG	NE	Yes	65	Imm.	0.04	0.31	.		0.09	.	-0.29	
Lippincott										62	follow up	0.33	0.37	.		-0.04	.	0.66	.
Orton-Gillingham										58	follow up	-0.47	-0.19			-0.81		-0.4	
48 - Snider, 1990																			
Direct Instruction	Syn	Basal	SmG	1yr.(60m/d)	1st	N	Mid	NE	No	66	follow up	0.38		0.6	0.44	0.1		.	.
51 - Torgesen et al., 1999																			
Lindamood PA	Syn	Rg.cls.	Tutor	2.5 yrs.(80m/- wk)	K	AR	NG	R	No	65	Imm.	0.33	0.08	.			0.58		
Embedded	LU	Rg.cls.	Tutor	2.5 yrs.(80m/- wk)	K	AR	NG	R	No	68	Imm.	0.32	0.52			.	0.12	.	
Lindamood PA										65	2nd yr.tr.	0.75	0.64	.		0.49	1.13		
Embedded										68	2nd yr.tr.	0.28	0.24			0.29	0.31		
Lindamood PA										65	3rd yr.tr.	0.67	0.67		0.64	0.36	1.01	.	
Embedded										68	3rd yr.tr.	0.17	0.25		0.1	0.17	0.16	.	

Appendix G (continued)

	Characteristics of Training				Characteristics of Part.				Features of Design			Effect Sizes on Post-tests							
Author and Year, Treatment	Type of Phonics	Control Group	Tr.unit	Length of Training	Grade/ Age	Reading Ability	SES	Group Assign.	Sig Pre-test Diff	Total N	Time of Post-test	Mean	Word ID	Dec	Spell	Comp	Nonw	Oral Read	Gen. Read
52 - Traweek & Berninger, 1997																			
Direct Instruction	Syn	Wh.L.	Class	1yr.	1st	AR	Low	NE	Y/Adj	38	Imm.	0.07	0.07						
53 - Tunmer & Hoover, 1993																			
RRD-Phonograms	LU	Rg.cls.	Tutor	42 s (30m/d)	1st	AR	NG	NG	NG	64	Imm.	3.71	2.94		1.63		1.49	8.79	
54 - Vandervelden & Siegel, 1997																			
Developmental	Misc	Rg.cls.	SmG	12wks(30–45m/wk)	K	AR	Low	NE	No	29	Imm.	0.47	0.04		1.11		0.57	0.15	
55 - Vickery et al., 1987																			
Orton-Gillingham	Syn	Rg.cls.	Class	1 yr.(55 m/d)	3rd	N	NG	NE	NG	63	Imm.	0.04							0.04
Orton-Gillingham	Syn	Rg.cls.	Class	1 yr.(55 m/d)	4th	N	NG	NE	NG	71	Imm.	0.04							0.04
Orton-Gillingham	Syn	Rg.cls.	Class	1 yr.(55 m/d)	5th	N	NG	NE	NG	74	Imm.	0.61							0.61
Orton-Gillingham	Syn	Rg.cls.	Class	1 yr.(55 m/d)	6th	N	NG	NE	NG	79	Imm.	0.43							0.43
Orton-Gillingham	Syn	Rg.cls.	Class	1 yr.(55 m/d)	3rd	LA	NG	NE	NG	46	Imm.	0.63							0.63
Orton-Gillingham	Syn	Rg.cls.	Class	1 yr.(55 m/d)	4th	LA	NG	NE	NG	47	Imm.	0.19							0.19
Orton-Gillingham	Syn	Rg.cls.	Class	1 yr.(55 m/d)	5th	LA	NG	NE	NG	45	Imm.	-0.2							-0.2
Orton-Gillingham	Syn	Rg.cls.	Class	1 yr.(55 m/d)	6th	LA	NG	NE	NG	41	Imm.	0.13							0.13
57 - Wilson & Norman, 1998																			
Sequential phonics	Syn	Wh.L.	Class	1 yr.	2nd	N	NG	NE	No	54	Imm.	-0.47	-0.33			-0.61			

Appendix G (continued)

Author and Year, Treatment	Type of Phonics	Control Group	Tr.unit	Length of Training	Grade/ Age	Reading Ability	SES	Group Assign.	Sig Pre-test Diff	Total N	Time of Post-test	Mean	Word ID	Dec	Spell	Comp	Nonw	Oral Read	Gen. Read
				Characteristics of Training															
59 - Freppon, 1991																			
Sequential phonics	Misc	Wh.L.	Class	1 yr.	1st	N	Mid	NE	Yes	24	Imm.	0						0	
60 - Griffith et al., 1992																			
Traditional basal	Misc	Wh.L.	Class	1 yr.	1st	N	NG	NE	No	24	Imm.	-0.33	-1.11		-0.54	-0.43	0.78		
69 - Umbach et al., 1989																			
Direct Instruction	Syn	Basal	SmG	1 yr.(50 m/d)	1st	AR	Low	R	No	31	Imm.	1.19	1.3			1.08			
72 - Gersten et al., 1988																			
Direct Instruction	Syn	Rg.cls.	Class	4 yrs.	K	AR	Low	NE	No	101	4th yr tr	0.24			0.16	0.28			0.27
Direct Instruction	Syn	Rg.cls.	Class	3 yrs.	1st	AR	Low	NE	No	141	3rd yr. tr.	0			-0.12	0.11			0.02
74 - Stuart, 1999																			
Jolly Phonics	Syn	Wh.L.	Class	12 wks(60m/-d)	K	AR	Low	NE	Y/Adj	112	Imm.	0.73	0.56		1.11	0.36	0.9		
Jolly Phonics										112	follow up	0.28	0.11		0.5	0.31	-0.03	0.49	
75 - Lovett et al., (in press)																			
Dir. Instruction + Analogy	Com	Misc.	SmG	70h	6-13yr	RD	Var	R	NG	37	Imm.	0.6	0.36	1	0.15	0.27	1.22		
Analogy + Direct Instruction	Com	Misc.	SmG	70h	6-13yr	RD	Var	R	NG	32	Imm.	0.21	0.04	0.55	-0.2	0.12	0.52		
Lovett Direct Instruction	Syn	Misc.	SmG	70h	6-13yr	RD	Var	R	NG	40	Imm.	0.24	0.21	0.36	-0.19	0.42	0.42		
Lovett Analogy	LU	Misc.	SmG	70h	6-13yr	RD	Var	R	NG	42	Imm.	0.5	0.47	0.75	0.01	0.6	0.66		

Appendix G (continued)

Abbreviations Key

Following is a key to Appendix G.

Word ID = Word Identification	h = hour
Dec = Decoding	s = session(s)
Spell = Spelling	wks = weeks
Comp = Comprehension	gr = grade
Nonw = Nonword reading	M = mean
Oral Read = Oral reading	K = Kindergarten
Gen. Read = Generic reading	RD = Reading Disabled
Syn = Synthetic;	AR = At Risk
LU = Larger Units	LA = Low Achievement
Misc = Miscellaneous	NG = Not Given
Com = Combination	Var = Varied
Wh.W. = Whole Word	Mid = Middle class
Wh.L. = Whole Language	R = Random assignment
Rg. Cls. = Regular class	NE = Non Equivalent groups
SmG = Small group	Y/Adj = Yes, but means were adjusted for pretest differences
yr, = year	Imm. = Immediate
m = minutes	tr = training
m/d = minutes a day	*class was used as the unit of analysis

Appendix G (continued)

APPENDIX B:
STUDIES INCLUDED IN THE
NRP META-ANALYSIS

Studies included in the meta-analysis of the *National Reading Panel Report* on phonics can be found on p. 2–145 *Report of the National Reading Panel*.

[**Note:** Studies were assigned numbers during the screening process. This list, taken directly from the NRP report, is incorrectly labeled and includes studies I am guessing were not analyzed, as they are not included in Appendix G. Either Appendix G or this list is incorrect. This is the panel's error, not mine. E. G.]

62 Barr, R. 1972. "The Influence of Instructional Conditions on Word Recognition Errors." *Reading Research Quarterly* 7(3): 509–29.

63 Barr, R. 1974. "The Effect of Instruction on Pupil Reading Strategies." *Reading Research Quarterly* 10(4): 555–82.

03 Blachman, B., D. Tangel, E. Ball, R. Black, and D. McGraw. 1999. "Developing Phonological Awareness and Word Recognition Skills: A Two-Year Intervention with Low-Income, Inner-City Children." *Reading and Writing: An Interdisciplinary Journal* 11: 273–93.

61 Blachowicz, C., L. McCarthy, and D. Ogle. 1979. "Testing Phonics: A Look at Children's Response Biases." *Illinois School Research and Development* 16(1): 1–6.

04 Bond, C., S. Ross, L. Smith, and J. Nunnery. 1995–96. "The Effects of the Sing, Spell, Read, and Write Program on Reading Achievement of Beginning Readers." *Reading Research and Instruction* 35: 122–141.

05 Brown, I., and R. Felton. 1990. "Effect of Instruction on Beginning Reading Skills in Children at Risk for Reading Disability." *Reading and Writing: An Interdisciplinary Journal* 2: 223–41.

64 Carnine, D. 1977. "Phonics Versus Look-Say: Transfer to New Words." *The Reading Teacher* 30: 636–40.

71 Carnine, D. 1980. "Phonics Versus Whole-Word Correction Proce-dures Following Phonics Instruction." *Education and Treatment of Children* 3(4): 323–29.

08 Eldredge, L. 1991. "An Experiment with a Modified Whole Language Approach in First-Grade Classrooms." *Reading Research and Instruc-tion* 30: 21–38.

09 Evans, M., and T. Carr. 1985. "Cognitive Abilities, Conditions of Learning, and the Early Development of Reading Skill." *Reading Re-search Quarterly* 20: 327–50.

11 Foorman, B., D. Francis, J. Fletcher, C. Schatschneider, and P. Mehta. 1998. "The Role of Instruction in Learning to Read: Preventing Read-ing Failure in At-Risk Children." *Journal of Educational Psychology* 90: 37–55.

12 Foorman, B., D. Francis, D. Novy, and D. Liberman. 1991. "How Letter-Sound Instruction Mediates Progress in First-Grade Reading and Spelling." *Journal of Educational Psychology* 83: 456–69.

13 Foorman, B., D. Francis, D. Winikates, P. Mehta, C. Schatschneider, and J. Fletcher. 1997. "Early Interventions for Children with Reading Disabilities. *Scientific Studies of Reading* 1: 255–76.

59 Freppon, P. 1991. "Children's Concepts of the Nature and Purpose of Reading in Different Instructional Settings." *Journal of Reading Be-havior* 23: 139–63.

15 Fulwiler, G., and P. Groff. 1980. "The Effectiveness of Intensive Phonics." *Reading Horizons* 21: 50–54.

72 Gersten, R., C. Darch, and M. Gleason. 1988. "Effectiveness of a Di-rect Instruction Academic Kindergarten for Low-Income Students." *The Elementary School Journal* 89: 227–40.

66 Gersten, R., T. Keating, and W. Becker. 1988. "The Continued Im-pact of the Direct Instruction Model: Studies Included in the Meta-Analysis Longitudinal Studies of Follow Through Students." *Education and Treatment of Children* 11(4): 318–27.

68 Gillon, G., and B. Dodd. 1997. "Enhancing the Phonological Pro-cessing Skills of Children with Specific Reading Disability." *European Journal of Disorders of Communication* 32: 67–90.

17 Gittelman, R., and I. Feingold. 1983. "Children with Reading Disorders—Efficacy of Reading Remediation." *Journal of Child Psy-chology and Psychiatry and Allied Disciplines* 24: 167–91.

18 Greaney, K., W. Tunmer, and J. Chapman. 1997. "Effects of Rime-Based Orthographic Analogy Training on the Word Recognition Skills

of Children With Reading Disability." *Journal of Educational Psychology* 89: 645–51.

60 Griffith, P., J. Klesius, and J. Kromey. 1992. "The Effect of Phonemic Awareness on the Literacy Development of First Grade Children in a Traditional or a Whole Language Classroom." *Journal of Research in Childhood Education* 6: 85–92.

22 Haskell, D., B. Foorman, and P. Swank. 1992. "Effects of Three Orthographic/Phonological Units on First-Grade Reading. *Remedial and Special Education* 13: 40–49.

73 Kameenui, E., M. Stein, D. Carnine, and A. Maggs. 1981. "Primary Level Word Attack Skills Based on Isolated Word, Discrimination List and Rule Application Training." *Reading Education* 6(2): 46–55.

26 Klesius, J., P. Griffith, and P. Zielonka. 1991. "A Whole Language and Traditional Instruction Comparison: Overall Effectiveness and Development of the Alphabetic Principle. Reading." *Research and Instruction* 30: 47–61.

28 Leach, D., and S. Siddall. 1990. "Parental Involvement in the Teaching of Reading: A Comparison of Hearing Reading, Paired Reading, Pause, Prompt, Praise, and Direct Instruction Methods." *British Journal of Educational Psychology* 60: 349–55.

29 Leinhardt, G., and M. Engel. 1981. "An Iterative Evaluation of NSR: Ripples in a Pond." *Evaluation Review* 5: 579–601.

75 Lovett, M., L. Lacerenza, S. Borden, J. Frijters, K. Steinbach, and M. DePalma. In press. "Components of Effective Remediation for Developmental Reading Disabilities: Combining Phonological and Strategy-Based Instruction to Improve Outcomes." *Journal of Educational Psychology*.

32 Lovett, R., M. Ransby, N. Hardwick, M. Johns, and S. Donaldson. 1989. "Can Dyslexia Be Treated? Treatment-Specific and Generalized Treatment Effects in Dyslexic Children's Reponse to Remediation." *Brain and Language* 37: 90–121.

33 Lovett, M., and K. Steinbach. 1997. "The Effectiveness of Remedial Programs for Reading Disabled Children of Different Ages: Does the Benefit Decrease for Older Children?" *Learning Disability Quarterly* 20: 189–210.

34 Lovett, M., P. Warren-Chaplin, M. Ransby, and S. Borden. 1990. "Training the Word Recognition Skills of Reading Disabled Children: Treatment and Transfer Effects." *Journal of Educational Psychology* 82: 769–80.

35 Lum, T., and L. Morton. 1984. "Direct Instruction in Spelling Increases Gain in Spelling and Reading Skills." *Special Education in Canada*, 58: 41–45.

36 Mantzicopoulos, P., D. Morrison, E. Stone, and W. Setrakian. 1992. "Use of the SEARCH/TEACH Tutoring Approach with Middle-Class Students at Risk for Reading Failure." *Elementary School Journal* 92: 573–86.

37 Marston, D., S. Deno, D. Kim, K. Diment, and D. Rogers. 1995. "Comparison of Reading Intervention Approaches for Students with Mild Disabilities." *Exceptional Children* 62: 20–37.

38 Martinussen, R., and J. Kirby. 1998. "Instruction in Successive and Phonological Processing to Improve the Reading Acquisition of At-Risk Kindergarten Children." *Developmental Disabilities Bulletin* 26: 19–39.

41 Oakland, T., J. Black, G. Stanford, N. Nussbaum, and R. Balise. 1998. "An Evaluation of the Dyslexia Training Program: A Multisensory Method for Promoting Reading in Students with Reading Disabilities." *Journal of Learning Disabilities* 31: 140–47.

65 Peterson, M., and L. Haines. 1992. "Orthographic Analogy Training with Kindergarten Children: Effects on Analogy Use, Phonemic Segmentation, and Letter-Sound Knowledge." *Journal of Reading Behavior* 24(1): 109–27.

44 Santa, C., and T. Hoien. 1999. "An Assessment of Early Steps: A Program for Early Intervention of Reading Problems." *Reading Research Quarterly* 34: 54–79.

47 Silberberg, N., I. Iversen, and J. Goins. 1973. "Which Remedial Reading Method Works Best?" *Journal of Learning Disabilities* 6: 18–27.

48 Snider, V. 1990. "Direct Instruction Reading with Average First-Graders." *Reading Improvement* 27:143–48.

74 Stuart, M. 1999. "Getting Ready for Reading: Early Phoneme Awareness and Phonics Teaching Improves Reading and Spelling in Inner-City Second Language Learners." *British Journal of Educational Psychology* 69: 587–605.

67 Torgesen, J., R. Wagner, and C. Rashotte. 1997. "Prevention and Remediation of Severe Reading Disabilities: Keeping the End in Mind." *Scientific Studies of Reading* 1(3): 217–34.

51 Torgesen, J., R. Wagner, C. Rashotte, E. Rose, P. Lindamood, T. Conway, and C. Garvan. 1999. "Preventing Reading Failure in Young Children with Phonological Processing Disabilities: Group and Indi-

vidual Responses to Instruction." *Journal of Educational Psychology* 91: 579–93.

52 Traweek, K., and V. Berninger. 1997. "Comparisons of Beginning Literacy Programs: Alternative Paths to the Same Learning Outcome." *Learning Disability Quarterly* 20: 160–68.

53 Tunmer, W., and W. Hoover. 1993. "Phonological Recoding Skill and Beginning Reading." *Reading and Writing: An Interdisciplinary Journal* 5: 161–79.

69 Umbacch, B., C. Darch, and G. Halpin. 1989. "Teaching Reading to Low Performing First Graders in Rural Schools: A Comparison of Two Instructional Approaches." *Journal of Instructional Psychology* 16: 23–30.

54 Vandervelden, M., and L. Siegel. 1997. "Teaching Phonological Processing Skills in Early Literacy: A Developmental Approach." *Learning Disability Quarterly* 20: 63–81.

55 Vickery, K., V. Reynolds, and S. Cochran. 1987. "Multisensory Teaching Approach for Reading, Spelling, and Handwriting, Orton-Gillingham Based Curriculum, in a Public School Setting." *Annals of Dyslexia* 37: 189–200.

57 Wilson, K., and C. Norman. 1998. "Differences in Word Recognition Based on Approach to Reading Instruction." *Alberta Journal of Educational Research* 44: 221–30.

REFERENCES

Allington, R. L. 1999. "Crafting State Educational Policy: The Slippery Role of Educational Research and Researchers." *Journal of Literacy Research* 31: 457–82.

Allington, R. L., and H. Woodside-Jiron. 1998a. "Decodable Texts in Beginning Reading: Are Mandates Based on Research?" *ERS Spectrum* 16(Spring): 3–11.

———. 1998b. "30 Years of Research . . . : When Is a Research Summary Not a Research Summary?" In *In Defense of Good Teaching: What Teachers Need to Know about the Reading Wars*, edited by K. Goodman, 143–57. York, ME: Stenhouse.

———. 1999. "The Politics of Literacy Teaching: How 'Research' Shaped Educational Policy." *Educational Researcher* 28(8), 4–13.

Bush, G. W. 2001. *No Child Left Behind*. Washington, DC: United States Department of Education.

———. 2001. Business Wire press release. Washington, DC, Tuesday, January 23.

Coles, G. 2000. *Misreading Reading: The Bad Science That Hurts Children*. Portsmouth, NH: Heinemann.

———. In press. *Misguided Research*. Portsmouth, NH: Heinemann.

Cunningham, J. 2001. "Essay Book Review: The National Reading Panel Report." *Reading Research Quarterly* 36(3): 326–35.

Dommel, F. William, and D. Langenberg. Press release, April 13, 2000. Available at *www.nationalreadingpanel.org*.

Ehri, L. 2000. Interview. In "National Reading Panel Report: Work Praised, but Distortion Fears Persist." *Reading Today* (June/July): 1.

Ehri, L., and S. Stahl. 2001. "Beyond the Smoke and Mirrors: Putting Out the Fire." *Phi Delta Kappan*. (September): 17–20.

Freeman, Y., and D. Freeman. 1996. *Teaching Reading and Writing in Spanish in the Bilingual Classroom*. Portsmouth, NH: Heinemann.

Garan, E. 2001. "Beyond the Smoke and Mirrors: A Critique of the National Reading Panel Report on Phonics." *Phi Delta Kappan* (March): 500–506.

———. 2001. "What Does the Report of the National Reading Panel Really Tell Us About Teaching Phonics?" *Language Arts Journal* (September): 59–67.

———. 2001. "More Smoking Guns: A Response to Linnea Ehri and Steven Stahl." *Phi Delta Kappan* (September): 21–27.

———. 2001. "Response to Timothy Shanahan." *Language Arts Journal* (September): 71.

Haab, L. 2001. Letter published on literacyforall listserve. Published with permission.

Kohn, A. 2000. *The Case Against Standardized Testing: Raising the Scores, Ruining the Schools*. Portsmouth, NH: Heinemann.

Krashen, S. 1982. *Principles and Practice in Second Language Acquisition*. New York: Prentice Hall.

———. 1985. *The Input Hypothesis*. Beverly Hills, CA: Laredo.

———. 1992. *Fundamentals of Language Education*. Beverly Hills, CA: Laredo.

———. 1999. *Three Arguments Against Whole Language & Why They Are Wrong*. Portsmouth, NH: Heinemann.

———. 2001. "More Smoke and Mirrors: A Critique of the National Reading Panel (NRP) Report on 'Fluency.' " *Phi Delta Kappan* 83(2): 118–21.

Moats, L. 2001. "Why Johnny Can't Spel." *People Weekly*, 27 August: 111–12.

Neuman, S. 2001. Press release. "Access to Print: Problem, Consequences, and Day One Instructional Solutions." White House Summit on Early Childhood Cognitive Development, Department of Education. Washington, DC, 27 July.

Neuman, S., and D. Celano. 2001. "Access to Print in Low-Income and Middle-Income Communities." *Reading Research Quarterly* 36(Jan/Feb/Mar): 8–26.

Neuman, S., and K. Roskos. 1997. "Literacy Knowledge in Practice: Contexts of Participation for Young Writers and Readers. *Reading Research Quarterly* (32): 10–32.

Ohanian, S. 1999. *One Size Fits Few: The Folly of Educational Standards*. Portsmouth, NH: Heinemann.

Report of the National Reading Panel: Teaching Children to Read. Report of the Subgroups. 1999. Washington, DC: National Institute of Child Health and Human Development.

Report of the National Reading Panel: Teaching Children to Read: Summary Booklet. 1999. Washington, DC: National Institute of Child Health and Human Development.

Report of the National Reading Panel: Teaching Children to Read. Publicity Video. 1999. Washington, DC: National Institute of Child Health and Human Development.

Rosenblatt, L. 1938. *Literature as Exploration.* New York: Appleton Century.

———. 2001. "Democracy and Education: Losing the Battle." Presentation at Rosenblatt AERA Convention, July, Seattle, Washington.

Routman, R. 1988. *Transitions.* Portsmouth, NH: Heinemann.

Samuels, S. J. 1984. Editorial. *Reading Research Quarterly* 19: 390–92.

Scribner, S., and M. Cole. 1981. *The Psychology of Literacy.* Cambridge, MA: Harvard University Press.

Shanahan, T. 2001. "Response to Elaine Garan: Teaching Should Be Informed by Research, Not Authoritative Opinion." *Language Arts Journal* 79(1): 71–72.

Stanovich, K. 1986. "Matthew Effects in Reading: Some Consequences of Individual Differences in the Acquisition of Literacy." *Reading Research Quarterly* (21): 360–406.

Taylor, D. 1998. *Beginning to Read and the Spin Doctors of Science: The Political Campaign to Change America's Mind About How Children Learn to Read.* Urbana, IL: National Council of Teachers of English.

"U.S. Secretary of Education Rod Paige Addresses IRA Conferees." 2001. *Reading Today* (June/July):21.

Yatvin, J. 2000. "Minority View." In *The Report of the National Reading Panel: Teaching Children to Read.* Washington, DC: National Institute of Child Health and Human Development.

INDEX